BAKE IT

One pan, over 90
unbeatable recipes
and a lot of fun

SLICE IT

Tom Oxford & Oliver Coysh

EAT IT

photography by Sam A Harris

quadrille

With thanks to everyone who's put up
with our shit since 2011: the staff,
family, friends and customers who've
had our backs since day one.

Tom & Oliver

Managing Director Sarah Lavelle
Senior Commissioning Editor Céline Hughes
Commissioning Editor Stacey Cleworth
Assistant Editor Sofie Shearman
Designer Alicia House
Brand Consultant Will Perrens (ATWORK)
Photographer Sam A Harris
Illustrator Ailsa Johnson
Food Stylist Becks Wilkinson
Prop Stylist Faye Wears
Head of Production Stephen Lang
Production Controller Sabeena Atchia

Published in 2022 by Quadrille Publishing
Limited

Quadrille
52–54 Southwark Street
London SE1 1UN
quadrille.com

Cataloguing in Publication Data: a catalogue
record for this book is available from the
British Library.

This book is not intended as a substitute for
genuine medical advice. Where allergens
are concerned, the reader should consult
a medical professional in matters relating
to ingredients, particularly with regard to
nut, gluten and dairy allergies.

ISBN 978 1 78713 866 7
Reprinted in 2022, 2023, 2024 (twice)
10 9 8 7 6 5

Text © Thomas Oxford & Oliver Coysh 2022
Photography © Sam A Harris 2022
Illustrations © Ailsa Johnson 2022
Design and layout © Quadrille 2022

Printed in China using vegetable-based inks

MIX
Paper | Supporting
responsible forestry
FSC® C018179

INTRODUCTION: TRIALS AND TRIBULATIONS OF BAKING PAST

We're Tom and Ollie, and we've been friends for over a quarter of a century. We started out making trouble at school, before graduating to making cakes instead. Over the last 11 years, we've managed to build a company together, which has turned us into complete divas and rendered us both unemployable. So what else is there to do, but plough on, and lend our hand to being authors of our very own baking book?

We first fired up The Exploding Bakery ovens back in 2011. It was off-the-cuff business planning, based on our desire to build a cake revolution! The 'real bread' campaign had stolen a march on us, and cake was the chubby kid left running behind. We felt real cake needed to step into the limelight. It needed a punk edge, a form of counterculture to push back against the existing pop music for sweet bakes. We wanted to knock off the rainbow sprinkles, set fire to the pink fondant icing and let all the unicorn cakes burn to the ground in a blaze of glory. We also knew that underneath the pink veneer of these mainstream cakes lurked some terrible ingredients: luxuries like proper butter and real chocolate were absent. With good intentions, we got to work creating recipes that go beneath the surface and focus on the integrity of the cake – creating knockout flavours and banging textures with killer ingredients at the same time. Along the way, though, we had to remind ourselves that one of the beauties cake offers us is escapism from reality: a respite from the daily grind, a sweet celebration and a little win with some sugar on the side. A hardcore punk movement was not the answer: we simply needed to make delicious things and have fun. If we did that, then cake revolution would surely follow.

Our tiny café was the melting pot that started this sweet and sticky rebellion. It doubled up as a wholesale bakery supplying other local cafés and delis, and customers queued for coffee while they watched the theatre of baking buzz in the background. We had a giant second-hand oven that huffed and puffed in the corner, churning out cakes that we stacked to the rafters. The original oven, nicknamed Biggie, still serves all our customers in the café today. Although a bit rough around the edges, it's a portal back to the early days: a reminder that we were flying by the seats of our pants with second-hand equipment and a business plan that would fit on the back of a spatula. Today, we bake our wholesale cakes in a more serious commercial kitchen that boasts some shiny new kit – we still have some of the original equipment kicking around as an ode to our baking roots. We may have grown up a little, but the music still thumps out of the speakers and the beers are prone to appearing on a Friday afternoon. We're constantly creating new recipes and sourcing better ingredients. Nationally, there has been a positive shift and improvement in baking, and we hope this continues.

WHY 'THE EXPLODING BAKERY'?
At the time, naming the company felt super important – and it probably was, to some degree. After a while though, to your staff, friends, family and customers, the name just becomes a sound that represents the company's values. We agonized over it like we were naming our first child, mostly over drinks at the local pub. The Exploding Bakery stuck with us from the moment we first stumbled on it. We were looking for something with energy and a little bit of danger and, most importantly, something that encapsulated the chemistry of baking: the colliding of ingredients and heat and the explosion of flavours this creates. We loved the idea of using a verb; 'exploding' gave our name energy, conjuring visuals for people to create their own idea of what we do. It also made people ask why, and challenged us to maintain the adventure and energy the name deserves.

ABOUT THIS BOOK

In this book, we've shared a streamlined set of recipes to help you delve into our world of baking without breaking the bank. There's no need to fill your cupboards with expensive equipment, surplus baking trays (sheet pans) and fancy gadgets. We believe in stripped-back baking: no faffing around with fancy decorating, just a dedication to flavour and texture in one tray.

This book belongs in the kitchen, living the cake-spattered life; we hope to see its pages sullied with buttery fingers and bookmarked with cake batter, knowingly falling open on your favourite recipe time and time again. We encourage creativity in baking, so make the recipes your own: add your own twist on things or improve the foundation that we've laid. If we find out this book is sitting unused on your shelf of colour-coded misery, we'll come around and snap your wooden spoons in two.

BAKING EQUIPMENT

We like to keep it simple on the equipment front, focusing on the ingredients and the method more than the gadgets. Sure, some hardcore patisserie requires niche equipment, but that's not what this book is about. We're all about getting stuck in and not stressing too much about the faff. There are a few things that will be essential though, so here we've shared a list of the bits of kit we've come to rely on. Invest in these and they will serve you well: not just for this book, but in your kitchen adventures for years to come. Filling your kitchen with luxuries is not essential when it comes to making banging bakes; most of the time, more analogue tools can get the job done. A balloon whisk, a sharp knife and some elbow grease are perfectly good substitutes for most fancy gadgets. The tray that all our recipes are based on is a vital investment: not only is it great for cakes, it can be used for all sorts of other dishes, like mac 'n' cheese, Saturday's bacon and Sunday's roast dinners.

THE TRAY

We have used exactly the same style of baking tray (sheet pan) every day since we started out in 2011; it's become part of the fabric of our cake designs, and really feels like part of the family. Of course, we have more than one. In fact, we've got them coming out of our ears: shiny new ones for the bakers to sully, rusty old ones stashed away for rainy days, and even some that have been repurposed as plant pots or screen stands in the office.

The tray in question is made by Wilton and measures 22 x 33 x 5cm (8½ x 13 x 2in). It can easily be found online, or, of course, you can choose another brand of tray in the same size. Do try to get as close to this size as possible, though, as all the recipes are based on it. We believe that steel is best, as aluminium tends to warp and conduct heat differently.

LINING THE TRAY

Here's a speedy trick for lining these trays with baking parchment: buy two and stack them with a sheet of paper in-between. The tray on top will push the parchment into place, lining the tray on the bottom. Plus, having two means you can double up on recipes or make sandwich or sheet cakes.

Baking in a round cake pan or deep loaf pan will deliver different results, and you'll need to adjust the cooking times and adapt our recipes accordingly. If you wish to do this, be our guest – just don't come at us all lawyered up when things don't go to plan.

DIGITAL SCALES

These are about as important as it gets in the baking world. Measuring by volume is a recipe for disaster and not to be trusted: anyone who says cups are OK is probably a cup salesman on commission. Scales are the best way to stay accurate and make sure you're starting off on the right foot. Digital scales are best, but old-fashioned weighted ones are fine as long as they're well looked after and occasionally calibrated.

STAND MIXERS AND OTHER OPTIONS

A top-of-the-range stand mixer will need a lot of use to earn its keep on your countertop. Perhaps if you're an accomplished baker and will use it daily for mixing dough and such things, then it's worth the investment. If not, there are plenty of affordable mixers available that are appropriate for more fair-weather bakers. All the recipes in this book can be made by hand but, for most, a basic stand mixer would make life easier; if you don't have one, there are other options that will work just as well. You can use an electric hand mixer with a very large bowl (see page 8), or, if you're really strapped for cash, a stick blender with a whisk attachment can do the job just fine. There's also the elbow grease method (just you, a bowl and a wooden spoon), which is fun, but hard work on the arms and can result in less consistent mixes.

MIXING BOWL

Bowls are bowls really, all dome-shaped and hollow, like a plate that hugs your food. If you're using a stand mixer, it will come with a mixing bowl; this is usually what we're referring to in the recipes. If you're using a hand mixer or the elbow-grease method, we recommend a heavy mixing bowl, one that won't spin out of control on the surface when you're going hell for leather to whip up some cream. Apart from that, it's just a matter of preference, really. Glass and ceramic bowls are nice, and so is the nostalgia of those beige patterned ones. The only important thing is that they can both withstand heat and conduct it when you're using them as part of a bain-marie (see right) to melt chocolate and butter.

FOOD PROCESSOR

As with the stand mixer, we think it's best to stay away from the pricier end of the spectrum, because when they break – which they do – the replacement parts are extortionate. We made these recipes using a fairly cheap food processor, and it got the job done no problem, so just get whatever you can afford. If you're into manual grating and don't need a food processor to do it for you, then a jug blender, Vitamix or NutriBullet might suit your needs better. They also double up nicely for a post-baking frozen margarita.

BOX GRATER

Some food processors do have grater attachments, but a box grater is probably more efficient unless you're feeding an entire army. Most of the time, if we call for ingredients to be grated, we're thinking of the coarse grating side of the grater. If we're talking lemons, though, a fine microplane will give you better zesting opportunities. That said, most box graters have a fine grating side, which is OK, although often a little blunt.

SPATULA

Probably the most undervalued tool in the kitchen. A silicone spatula will help you out of many sticky situations, and is a great tool for thoroughly scraping out the mixing bowl. Not only does this reduce waste – quite often there's up to 100g (3½oz) of cake mix still clinging to the bowl – it also makes things easier when it comes to washing-up.

OVEN

Like people, every oven has its own personality, but once you get to know them, their quirks are easier to manage. An oven thermometer can help you with getting an accurate temperature reading, but only you can work out your own oven's particular hot spots and the solutions to these frustrations, like turning things around halfway through baking or dropping the heat towards the end of a bake. This is why the oven temperatures we give in this book are just a guide: 160°C (320°F) could be more like 180°C (350°F) if you have a feisty element. So get to know your oven, take it out for dinner a few times and tame the beast. The majority of ovens are now fan-assisted, so the recipes have been written with these in mind. If your oven is different, you're the best person to calculate timings and temperatures.

BAIN-MARIE

Not necessarily a specialist piece of equipment: this is simply some water in a pan with a bowl on top. It's a gentle way to bring heat to an ingredient and warm it up. We use this method for melting butter and chocolate, although a microwave will do a similar job. If you like, you can use the bowl from the stand mixer and just place it over a pan of simmering water, rather than using separate bowls and creating extra washing-up.

Note: When tempering chocolate, it's a good idea to make sure the water isn't touching the bowl. If you prefer, you can melt or temper chocolate directly in a pan with a thick, heavy base over a very gentle heat; just make sure you keep things moving with a spatula.

HEAVY-BASED SAUCEPAN

We use this term a lot in our recipes. A cast-iron pan with an enamel coating is perfect, as it will warm up gently, helping to evenly distribute the heat. A stainless-steel pan with a very thick bottom is good too. Try to avoid using pans with thin bases, unless it's pancake day.

DIGITAL THERMOMETER

If you do want to make some of the more technical recipes, like Pâtes de Fruits (page 147) or French Caramel (page 149), you will need one of these. With some experience, you might get away with not using one, but they really are a helpful tool. We advise getting one with a long, heat-resistant cable with the probe on the end: this means you don't have to stick your hand in a bubbling pot of boiling sugar and run the risk of burns. You can also use the probe for roasting joints of meat to perfection or sizzling up a knockout steak that cuts like butter.

KNIVES

Probably the most used tool in any kitchen. We use the Victorinox serrated pastry knife, which is designed for bakers and cuts cakes without making lots of crumbs. It can also be used to chop vegetables, slice tomatoes, cut bread and carve the thinnest slices of ham. The black plastic handle doesn't make it the prettiest of things, but they do also come in rosewood for a more dashing look. Do note, there's no pointy end, so you will probably need another knife as its henchman. The little Opinel paring knives are really great for intricate dissection and peeling.

SILICONIZED BAKING PARCHMENT

Not only does this save on the messy job of greasing up trays that would probably end up with half the cake sticking to them anyway, it also saves on washing-up. It's excellent for lining any metallic tray destined for the oven, or laying over that garlic-infused chopping board when it's time to cut and serve your cake. It can even be used for wrapping up your bakes to take to a friend, but make sure to tie it up with string rather than sticky tape, as the tape won't adhere to it. If you can't get hold of siliconized parchment, you'll need to butter some regular baking parchment to make it non-stick. It's best to avoid foil when it comes to lining baking trays (sheet pans).

INGREDIENTS:
BANG FOR YOUR BUCK

This is about getting the right ingredients for the job at hand, making sure they are used in the right way and giving you a better understanding of their purpose. We understand that not everyone is able to saunter down to the local farmers' market; it's more likely you'll be hitting the supermarket and fitting it into your lifestyle. We do believe there are a few ingredients where you'll really feel the gains if you trade up, though, so hear us out.

SALT

Salt often doesn't get the recognition it deserves in the larder of baking ingredients: this little mineral is responsible for putting the wind in your flavour sails. Unless we state otherwise in the recipe, assume it's a fine sea salt being used. We'll occasionally specify flaked sea salt for sprinkling on top of the cakes. We're really into Halen Môn sea salt, but there are lots of other brands worth using.

GROUND ALMONDS

This is a type of nut flour, sometimes called almond meal. Using a finely ground nut meal will add so much flavour and texture to your bake. It will also help lock in moisture to prolong the shelf life. No more dry cake for you!

NUTS

Some of the recipes give instructions for how to deal with nuts with their husks on: buying blanched nuts will save you this process. The bitterness from the nut husk can add flavour, so it's completely up to you whether you leave it in. The best nut suppliers we've found in the UK are Food & Forest, who mainly work with regenerative farms to produce nuts that you'll want to show to all your friends. Do a bit of research and try and find the best supplier in your area.

CHOCOLATE

When we say chocolate, we don't mean just any old chocolate. We take it seriously and expect others to do the same. People need to understand what's good and what's bad in the chocolate industry. For too long, we've been sold bars that are low-grade, slave-made and planet-harming. Sure, they might taste sweet and familiar, but the best chocolate transcends those basic flavour profiles, bringing in fruity caramels and nutty earthiness, and even hints of smokiness and coffee. So choose well and it will add myriad layers of flavour to a simple brownie or ganache. Some cocoa butter is a good thing when it comes to baking, so it's best to avoid anything that's 75 per cent cocoa solids or more, as the resulting bake will be too dry. We work directly with a Colombian company called Casa Luker who grow high-grade cacao. Most importantly, they're slavery-free and have pledged not to cut down the rainforest. There are other companies doing similar things, so check the credentials and it will pay off, both in flavour and in your levels of smugness for saving the world.

EGGS

Most of us know the importance of buying local and organic, so we don't want to preach about this. A good egg will give you better baking results, and really fresh eggs can lend lightness to your cakes. By whipping some air into the mix, your eggs bring a slight lift to your bake in a soufflé fashion. Unhappy chickens will produce sorry eggs and make sad cakes. Please don't keep your eggs in the fridge; if you do, get them out the day before you use them. We use medium-sized eggs in all the recipes because the contents of a medium-sized egg weigh 50g (1¾oz), making it easier to calculate adjustments and ratios.

BUTTER

This is the crème de la crème – literally. Butter is the fat from the cream, and is an absolute luxury, not a commodity used only for spreading on toast. It's actually not that difficult to make your own butter using fresh cream, and you can use the resulting buttermilk in lots of different recipes.

Salted or unsalted? Well, most baking books and recipes will tell you to use unsalted, so you can control the amount of salt in the recipe. In true Exploding Bakery fashion, these rules don't apply here – we use salted butter. It's a tad more work to calculate the amount of salt needed, but the advantage of using salted butter is that you don't need to keep it in the fridge, as it will last for a couple of weeks at room temperature. Unsalted butter, on the other hand, needs to be used within a few days when kept at ambient temperatures. Salted butter is normally 2 per cent salt, so a 250g (9oz) packet will contain 5g salt – about a teaspoon.

OIL

When it comes to oils, we've found that a fairly neutral flavour is the best for baking, which is why we use rapeseed (canola) oil, in most of our recipes, although sunflower oil works well too. The exception to this rule is when you want it to add to the flavour, in which case, you might want to use coconut oil, olive oil or cold-pressed oils, which can carry a lot of bitterness and a peppery, complex flavour. When it comes to measuring oil, it's much more accurate to weigh it: a good rule of thumb is that it weighs 10 per cent less than its volume. For example, 200ml (7fl oz) of oil would weigh 180g (6⅓oz).

FLOUR

When it comes to quality flour, there's a really encouraging movement towards heritage grains in the UK right now, and small-scale growers are seeing the benefits of stepping away from mono crops. Besides being a change that is needed on a mass scale, it's bringing some really interesting grains to the table. They're much more flavoursome and have better textures, and the fact that they are wholegrain and stone-ground makes them so much healthier for you. If you can get hold of a bag of heritage flour, we encourage you to add some to the recipes here: swapping out just 20 per cent of the plain (all-purpose) flour will bring a different dimension to your bake and help with the push for more sustainable crops.

Sifting is an essential part of baking: not only does it aerate the flour, it gets rid of clumps and separates the particles, which allows the flour to mix with the other ingredients more evenly. There's a simple joy to sifting flour: get a bit of rhythm tapping the sieve, jiggle the hips and cascade that wheat to the beat.

When we refer to plain flour in recipes, we mean an all-purpose white flour with a lower protein level than a strong bread flour. Cake doesn't want strong gluten bonds forming, as this would create a heavy bake. We sometimes use self-raising flour: this is just plain flour with a raising agent already mixed in. You can make your own to get more control if you're confident: it's roughly 1 teaspoon of baking powder per 100g (3½oz) of flour, which is about 5 per cent baking powder.

VANILLA

Although completely ubiquitous, vanilla is actually one of the most expensive and labour-intensive ingredients in the world. With this in mind, it's important not to waste any of that delicate little bean. One way to be sure of this is to keep the husks and leave them languishing in your sugar bowl to infuse the grains with some added aroma. If you like a shortcut, then we recommend vanilla paste; failing that, a bottle of extract brings the bouquet needed to animate your bakes. At the bakery, we've been using Little Pod Vanilla since day one, and they get our seal of approval. And what of vanilla essence? It's a disingenuous imitation and nothing like the real deal.

CREAM CHEESE

Here's a note on cream cheese etiquette. With its slightly obdurate yet silken texture, Philadelphia is the undisputed champion when it comes to making a topping. However, it does have a habit of buckling under the heat of the oven and becoming a bit too runny. So, for a baked cheesecake or cream cheese brownie, we'd recommend going with the supermarket own-brand stuff: it's a little less smooth, but tends to hold firm in the oven and doesn't throw its curds out of the pram.

OATS

We've found that blending rolled (porridge) and jumbo oats gives you the right structure and texture for the perfect flapjack. Oats are naturally gluten-free, although they're often milled in the same place as other grains containing gluten, so there is a bit of cross contamination. We like to use gluten-free oats if we're baking for anyone with gluten intolerances. Obviously, if this doesn't concern you, you don't need to bother with the gluten-free kind. If the recipe calls for oatmeal and you can't find any, just blitz up some oats in a food processor until they take on a powdery form.

POLENTA (CORNMEAL)

As with oats, we like to blend our polenta to get a better structure and texture. We go for a mix of fine-milled and medium. The really coarse kind will be very grainy in a cake, so we avoid it. If this is all you can get, though, pre-soaking it can help soften the bite.

RAISING AGENTS

Bicarbonate of soda (baking soda) and baking powder are the usual culprits for giving cake a lift. It's a good idea to go easy on these, though, as using too much can leave a nasty taste in the mouth. Baking powder is just bicarb with acid, which sets it off and creates CO_2 within the cake as it heats up. If you're using bicarbonate of soda on its own, you'll need some acid to get it working properly; adding some lemon juice to your cake mix does the trick. Good, fresh eggs can really help lighten cakes too, and whipping some air into them during the mixing process will aid the elevation.

BAKING TIPS

A PINCH OF SALT

All recipes should be taken with a pinch of salt. When it comes to baking in particular, the variables are too great for these scientific methods to be replicated with absolute accuracy, so don't panic. It's best to let go of your baking anxieties and put yourself in the hands of the baking gods, as they ultimately roll the dice on the outcome.

Even though we've been baking away for years, honing our consistency, methods and ingredients, we still find that every bake is unique. It could be that one baker's mixing technique is slightly different from another's, or that one of the ovens decided to play it cool for a day and drop its temperature by a few degrees. The conditions are constantly changing, but ultimately, something delicious always emerges. We've come to terms with the fact that ours is a handmade product, and with that comes daily variance. It will happen with your bakes, too, so there's no reason to worry when things don't go exactly to plan. It happens to everyone.

A recipe is little more than a guide, so it's best to assume that the person who wrote it doesn't know the variables in your kitchen or of the particular ingredients you'll be using. Your fruit could have a much higher acidity, making the raising agents react quicker. Your flour could be more finely ground, creating a greater surface area, which takes up more moisture and means you'll need to add a little more of your wet ingredients to avoid a dry cake. That's just two small things that you'll have minimal control over; then there's the obvious ones, like oven type or the water content of your ingredients. Simply lowering the temperature of a fan-assisted oven won't give you the same results as cooking in an oven without a fan. Some ovens retain the moisture of the bake better than others. Thermal dynamics plays a huge role, and the core temperature of the goods needs to reach a certain heat to become cooked (hopefully while the outside of the cake remains unburnt). There's also the conductivity of the tray to consider: steel, aluminium and silicone will all yield different results.

Even the weather can play a part in how your bake turns out. It's all enough to melt the mind, so it's best to not battle the variables too much. Instead, just accept that every bake is unique, like every person, and embrace the quirks of your cakes.

Cooking from a recipe is a way of learning: it's like a spell-check for cooking. Experienced cooks may not need recipes, because they have the skills, knowledge and experience to whip stuff up from memory, from their very own library of blueprints. However, baking is slightly different to cooking: sometimes it's hard to express yourself with flair and the panache of a chef. The structural engineering of the masterpiece needs thought, composure and planning. Bakers are more like architects than rock stars. Sometimes, quantities and measurements can be remembered, but most of the time, even the most seasoned baker will be required to check the recipe. This doesn't display anything other than the care required to produce the baked goods in their best possible form.

GET YOUR SH*T TOGETHER

If you want to avoid running around, frantically looking in cupboards and drawers, with chocolate smeared across your brow while the caramel slowly burns with every second you spend searching for the thermometer, here are a few wise words to prevent the chaos: a little planning goes a very long way when you're up to your elbows in cake mix.

Some professionals use the term 'mise en place'. This roughly translates to getting your sh*t together or getting everything in its place before you begin. It's really about having a little composure, weighing out all the ingredients beforehand and organizing them in the order they'll be used. Then sit down and read the recipe a few times, and think how the method will play out. Get all the equipment ready, check it's clean after sitting on top of a cupboard for six months, and more importantly, check it's working. Then you can get into the groove of things and enjoy the process without the stress.

A METHOD IN OUR MADNESS

Here are a few useful notes on the methods that feature in our recipes. They're little explainers on why we do things in a particular way and what we mean by certain phrases.

Emulsify

We use this term a lot in the recipe methods. Emulsification is just a fancy word for when the oils or fats bond with another liquid through mixing. This is usually aided by eggs and other dry ingredients to bring things together in a glossy mix. In time, you'll be able to hear the change in sound when something has emulsified, like a true Jedi baker.

Swapping out

You may notice that we introduce our recipes with the options of making alterations and going off-piste; this is based on how we've always baked in the past, and how useful or inspiring it can be to try swapping out an ingredient. We really want to encourage you to do this, as it will hopefully highlight that there is no right or wrong way of making something, instilling some self-confidence as you steer your own ship.

Scraping the bowl

In all recipes, it's a really good idea to use a spatula to scrape down the sides and bottom of the mixing bowl, during the mixing process, so that you can make sure everything gets incorporated and you don't end up with half your ingredients hiding at the bottom.

The oven

When we say 'place the cake in the oven', we always mean on the middle rack or shelf: this will give you the most even bake. However, if you're looking for a darker colour on the top of your cake and you're confident that it's already cooked in the middle, perhaps you're better off moving things up to the top rack to finish off. Or if the top of the cake is getting too dark and the middle still isn't cooked, cover the cake with foil and place it on the bottom rack. The temperatures given in the book all refer to fan-assisted ovens, so if you have a non-fan oven, you'll need to up the temperature by about 20°C (36°F) – but please remember what we said about variables and the quirks of individual ovens (see page 8).

Volume vs weight

Weighing ingredients is easier than trying to find the measurements on the side of a scratched-up jug, squinting as you hold it up to your face. It's more accurate, too, so for oil, we've provided both the volume in millilitres and the weight in grams and ounces. Do note that oil doesn't weigh in at 1kg per litre: it weighs less than water by about 10 per cent. And while we're on the subject of volume vs weight, when it comes to baking, cup measurements should be abolished: they're dated, inaccurate and far too open to interpretation. Our opinion is fact, so try to avoid them if you can. Digital scales sometimes have a bit of a lag time as well, so it's always good to add slowly, then let them catch up, especially if you're adding one ingredient to another in the same bowl.

Bain-marie

We like to use this method for melting or heating ingredients (although, as we mentioned on page 8, a microwave can do the job just as well if you give an ingredient short blasts with a stir between each nuking). Using a bain-marie is very simple – just make sure the pan isn't overfilled and the water isn't bubbling; a gentle heat is all that's required.

Butter

All the butter used in the recipes is room-temperature soft, unless specified otherwise. Sometimes you'll be required to fully melt the butter, other times you'll need it to be chilled before you get started; this will be detailed in the recipe.

Timings

Adding timings to a recipe can make you feel like you should be doing things faster or that you've rushed it; it's better to set aside a good amount of time and enjoy the process. Some cakes are quicker than others to make, and some are more technical and require a little more planning. We feel it's a little presumptuous to set amounts of time per recipe – aside from the baking times, of course – as some people are speed demons in the kitchen, while others prefer to take their sweet time.

Portion sizes

Unless otherwise specified, all the bakes in this book make about 16 large slices – but, of course, it's all down to your personal preference and how you slice them.

Cake cooling

It's perfectly fine to leave a cake in the baking tray (sheet pan) to cool. If you're in a rush, you can pop it in the freezer or place it by an open window: just be careful someone doesn't run off with it. It's important not to remove a cake from the tray while it's still piping hot, as it will be very delicate and can break. If you want to eat something when it's still warm, leave it in the tray for around 15 minutes, then carefully lift it out by holding the edge of the baking parchment on the longer sides to form a cradle, then place it on a flat surface and slice. Unless otherwise stated, our bakes are best enjoyed at room temperature, so if you store them in the fridge, let them come up to room temperature before eating.

A cherry on top

Adding a cherry on the top of a cake is a communication tool more than anything; it's something to catch the eye. Our rules for baking are to prioritize flavour, then texture and lastly aesthetic. Good cake shouldn't necessarily have to look fancy. However, cake, by its very nature, comes mostly in rather dull colours, usually occupying a spectrum of beige to brown. Cake is not a commodity – it's flippin' expensive when made properly – so the occasional bit of make-up is needed to entice your punters to take a bite, especially for those who don't quite understand the work that goes into it. Spoon-feeding the notion that this is something special does require a little work, and we find the addition of fruit can really add that splash of attention-grabbing, appetite-whetting colour. Showing off some technical skills with brittles, candied fruits and such things can add a bit of texture and appeal. Check out the Technical Section (pages 138–157), where you can learn a few extra skills on this subject.

KEY

Throughout the main chapters, all cake and brownie recipes are marked-up with the following labels, where relevant:

VEGAN
GLUTEN FREE
NUT FREE

Do check the labels of individual ingredients when preparing vegan, nut-free and gluten-free recipes, as manufacturing methods can vary.

BASIC BAKES

The recipes in this section are like stabilizers for your bike:
as you learn to ride, you can take them off and journey on towards
whatever part of the cake world your heart desires. Go with your
gut, and feed your baking dreams. To start with, we've got some
basic recipes for you to get under your belt: they should give
you the confidence to devise some of your own recipes, inject
some ideas into some of ours, and most importantly, kick-start
your baking so you can shout: 'Look, Mum! No hands.' Some of the
recipes here, like the Sponge Cake on page 24, are as basic as
it gets, but hopefully there's enough inspiration for you to get
creative and feel comfortable with designing your own concept.
The more you bake, the more instinct and intuition you'll gain.
This is what will make you a better baker.

BLUEBERRY SLICE

A simple yet punchy number that is greater than the sum of its parts, with the blueberries, sour cream and lemon all pulling in the same direction. To speed up the cooking time, a cupcake version of this recipe would work for sure.

TO MAKE THE CAKE
250g (9oz) caster
   (superfine) sugar, plus
   2 tablespoons for sprinkling
4 medium eggs
200ml (7fl oz) sour cream
juice of 1 lemon
100g (3½oz) melted butter
325g (11½oz) plain (all-purpose)
   flour
2 teaspoons baking powder
1 teaspoon salt
300g (10½oz) fresh blueberries

TO TOP
icing (confectioners') sugar, to dust
finely grated zest of 1 lemon

NUT FREE

Pictured overleaf.

Preheat the oven to 160°C fan/320°F/gas 4 and line your 22 x 33 x 5cm (8½ x 13 x 2in) baking tray (sheet pan), see page 7.

You can make the cake by hand or using a stand mixer; either works well. Start by beating together the sugar and eggs until pale and a little frothy, then add the sour cream and lemon juice and mix until well combined. Now add the melted butter and bring it all together slowly.

Sift the flour, baking powder and salt into a bowl and add to the wet mixture a little at a time while mixing slowly. Make sure to scrape down the sides of the bowl with a spatula and then mix again; this will ensure everything is evenly mixed.

Pour the batter into your lined tray and spread it out evenly with a spatula. Scatter the blueberries across the top, then sprinkle the 2 tablespoons of sugar over the blueberries. Bake for 50–55 minutes until the bake is golden, the blueberries are bursting and a knife comes out clean. Leave to cool in the tray, then dust generously with icing (confectioners') sugar and sprinkle your lemon zest over the top.

Best eaten while still a little warm. This will keep for another couple of days in an airtight container in the fridge.

If blueberries are out of season, you can use frozen ones. Raspberries would also work if you want to try using a different fruit.

CHOCOLATE BANANA TRAYBAKE

Stolen from our antipodean relations down under, this is usually baked in a loaf pan, but works brilliantly in a baking tray (sheet pan). The nuts add a really nice element of texture, but if you want to make this nut-free, just slice up an extra banana into coins and use that for the topping instead: a little sprinkling of sugar will add a nice sheen to these slices. This cake has quite a tight crumb, so add a teaspoon of baking powder if you want a lighter sponge. Like all banana breads, it's a great way of salvaging those last bananas in the fruit bowl that have a few fruit flies buzzing around; if you only have a couple, just unzip them from their skins and tuck them away in the freezer until you have enough to bake with. Make sure they're defrosted and at room temperature before using.

TO MAKE THE CAKE

570g (1lb 4oz) soft, ripe, brown bananas (peeled weight)
340g (12oz) caster (superfine) sugar
275ml (9fl oz) / (250g/9oz) sunflower or rapeseed (canola) oil
560g (1lb 3¾oz) self-raising flour
1 teaspoon salt
150g (5¼oz) dark chocolate, broken into pieces
375ml (12¾fl oz) unsweetened soy milk or oat milk

TO MAKE THE TOPPING

100g (3½oz) pecans
1 tablespoon golden or maple syrup

VEGAN

Pictured on page 21.

Turn on the oven to 160°C fan/320°F/gas 4 and line your 22 x 33 x 5cm (8½ x 13 x 2in) baking tray (sheet pan), see page 7.

Place the pecans in your lined tray and drizzle with the golden or maple syrup, then pop in the oven while it's heating up. After 5 minutes, check them, and turn them with a spatula to make sure the syrup has covered all the pecans. Give them 5 minutes more, then turn out on to a sheet of baking parchment and leave to cool. The syrup should be glistening but still runny: you don't want any caramelization on the nuts at this point, just a nice sheen.

To make the cake, mix the bananas with the sugar in a stand mixer, or a large mixing bowl, to create a sort of paste. Then slowly add the oil, while mixing, until the mixture emulsifies. Sift the flour and salt into a bowl, then add them to the banana mixture, along with the chocolate, and combine until everything is fully incorporated. Finally, add the soy milk and mix a little more until you have a runny batter. Pour the mixture into your tray, top with the syrupy nuts and bake for 50–60 minutes.

This cake is at its best when it's still warm, but it's also great cut into slices and toasted. It will keep for a week in an airtight container in the fridge.

If you feel like going the extra mile, check out the Technical Section and add the vegan Coconut Cream Icing on page 143.

LEMON DRIZZLE CAKE

Let's all just agree that a lemon drizzle cake is probably the best cake in the world. It has an iconic and quintessentially British appeal, from the WI tent at a balmy summer fête, to the gin-and-tonic fuelled garden party. I don't think I've ever turned down a slice of lemon drizzle, and I certainly don't ever intend to do so. This one is no exception to that rule: it's perfectly moist, with just the right balance of tart and sweet to keep you interested. The candied lemons are optional, I guess, but you'd be a fool not to add that extra razzle-dazzle to your lemmy drizz.

TO MAKE THE CAKE
375g (13¼oz) soft butter
500g (1lb 2oz) caster
  (superfine) sugar
6 medium eggs
finely grated zest of 3 lemons
500g (1lb 2oz) self-raising flour
1 teaspoon salt
180ml (6fl oz) whole milk

TO MAKE THE SYRUP
150g (5¼oz) caster sugar
50ml (1¾fl oz) water
juice of 1 lemon

TO MAKE THE ICING
300g (10½oz) icing
  (confectioners') sugar
about 75ml (2½fl oz) lemon juice
  (about 2 lemons' worth)

NUT FREE

Pictured on page 20.

Preheat the oven to 160°C fan/320°F/gas 4 and line your 22 x 33 x 5cm (8½ x 13 x 2in) baking tray (sheet pan), see page 7.

To make the cake, cream the butter and sugar until nice and light, then add the eggs and lightly beat. Now fold in your lemon zest, flour and salt, adding them a bit at a time. If you are using a mixer, do this on the lowest speed and make sure to scrape down the sides of the bowl between additions. Finally, add the milk, pouring it in slowly as you mix. Make sure everything is well combined and that you have scraped the edges and bottom of the bowl before giving it one final mix, then pour the batter into your prepared tray and bake for 45 minutes.

Meanwhile, get started on your syrup. Add the syrup ingredients to a heavy-based saucepan over a medium heat. Give it all a stir to dissolve the sugar, bring to the boil and then set aside. This should still be warm by the time the cake comes out of the oven so it will absorb into the sponge better.

To make the icing, sift the icing (confectioners') sugar into a bowl and mix in the lemon juice, adding it slowly and just a little at a time. A balloon whisk or even a fork is really good for this, and both will eventually smooth out any of those pesky sugary lumps. You might not want to add all of the juice; you need just enough to give you a thick pouring consistency, like lava, just as it's cooling down.

Your cake is ready when it has a golden top with a nice dome that springs back when you press it. Take it out of the oven and, using a toothpick or similar, dot little holes all over the top. Allow to cool for 10 minutes, then remove from the tray and transfer to a wire rack or chopping board and evenly pour the syrup over the top. When it has all soaked in, pour over the icing and let it run off the edges of the cake, gently ushering it to the sides with a spatula if you need to.

Best eaten once cool. This will keep for a week in an airtight container in the fridge.

If you'd like to top this cake with candied lemons, see our Quasi Candied Citrus recipe on page 156. Just make sure they are cool and the icing is set before you lay them on top, otherwise they will release moisture and slide about.

SPONGE CAKE

It's OK to be wearing the white karate belt around your apron right now; before long, you'll be climbing the ranks. Sponges are a fun starting point for understanding the balance of wet and dry ingredients. They're also fully adaptable, and can be made with yoghurt, buttermilk or different flours, such as buckwheat or oatmeal. There's scope for additions like lemon, vanilla and chocolate, and potentially dried or whole fruits too. Using cornflour (cornstarch) can help with sinking fruit or chocolate chips, and too much acidity can send your raising agents out of control, so keep this in mind when using things like lemon juice or even yoghurt. Once you've mastered the basic sponge, you'll have a canvas to become the artist you desire: paint a picture with creams and jams, cover with buttercream icing or chocolate ganache, and finish with sprinklings of nuts and seeds, or even dried or fresh flower petals if that floats your boat.

TO MAKE THE CAKE

300g (10½oz) soft butter
300g (10½oz) caster
 (superfine) sugar
6 medium eggs
150g (5¼oz) ground almonds
150g (5¼oz) plain (all-purpose)
 flour
1 teaspoon baking powder
1 teaspoon salt

TO MAKE THE TOPPING

400g (14oz) mascarpone
100g (3½oz) sour cream
10ml (2 teaspoons) vanilla extract
50g (1¾oz) icing (confectioners')
 sugar, sifted
15–20 fresh strawberries,
 thinly sliced

Preheat the oven to 160°C fan/320°F/gas 4 and line your 22 x 33 x 5cm (8½ x 13 x 2in) baking tray (sheet pan), see page 7.

To make the cake, ensure your butter is nice and soft, but not melted. Add it to the mixing bowl and cream together with the sugar, ideally using an electric whisk or stand mixer. The mixture should become paler the more you whisk. Add the eggs, one at a time, and combine until they've emulsified and the mixture is smooth and glossy. Add the ground almonds and beat with all your fury. If the mixture has split, fear not: the flour will bring it all together.

Sift in the flour, baking powder and salt, then gently fold it all together, either with a spatula or with the electric whisk or mixer on a very low speed. Pour the batter into your lined tray, level it out and bake for 35 minutes. The sponge should have domed nicely, and you'll know it's done if it springs back when you give it a light press. Turn the cake out of the tray, ideally on to a wire rack – if you don't have one, a chopping board will do.

While it's cooling, make the topping by whipping together the mascarpone, sour cream and vanilla, then fold in the sifted icing (confectioners') sugar. Spread this over the cooled sponge using a pallet knife or spatula, then lay the strawberry slices across the top, as neatly or artistically as suits your style.

Alternatively, you can split the mixture between two trays (600g/1lb 5oz in each) and bake for 20–25 minutes, then use the two sheets of sponge to make a sandwich cake, spreading a thin layer of icing over one cake, topping with the other cake, and then finishing with the rest of the icing and the strawberries on top.

Best eaten while still a little warm. This will keep for about 5 days in an airtight container in the fridge.

See the Technical Section (pages 138–157) for different icings and toppings. This also makes a very good Victoria sponge sandwich, with strawberry jam and buttercream in the middle, and a heavy snowfall of icing sugar on top.

CARAMELIZED NECTARINE CLAFOUTIS

Some cakes are just so simple, and all the better for it. I like to think of cakes like this as the omelette of the baking world: you can smash it out and use whatever fruit you have in the house, or whatever is going too soft to eat. We're using nectarines in this recipe, but in a different season you might want to use plums, cherries, rhubarb or mixed berries. You can cook the fruit in a little butter and sugar first, if you like, or in some liquor like kirsch, if you want to get a little boozy. Although it's a tad difficult to remove the stones, those rock-hard nectarines labelled 'ripen at home', which are usually good only for the bin, can serve a purpose in this cake – their sourness is welcome, as is their firmness and juice retention.

TO MAKE THE CUSTARD

80g (3oz) plain (all-purpose) flour
100g (3½oz) ground almonds
1 teaspoon baking powder
4 medium eggs
80g (3oz) caster (superfine) sugar
100ml (3½fl oz) whole milk
200ml (7fl oz) double (heavy) cream
1 teaspoon vanilla extract

TO MAKE THE FRUIT FILLING

8 nectarines (stoned and quartered)
100g (3½oz) light brown sugar
a pinch of ground cinnamon
65g (2¼oz) butter

icing (confectioners') sugar, for dusting

Preheat the oven to 180°C fan/350°F/gas 6 and line your 22 x 33 x 5cm (8½ x 13 x 2in) baking tray (sheet pan), see page 7.

Start with the custard. Mix together all the ingredients until you have a smooth batter; a stand mixer or a food processor would make life easier for this. It's a good idea to leave the batter to rest for at least an hour if you can. This helps swell the starch and relax the gluten, which gives a thicker but lighter texture, rather than a denser one.

While that's resting, prepare your nectarines (or whatever fruit you're using). Lay the nectarine quarters in your tray and sprinkle over the sugar and cinnamon, then dot over the butter. Pop in the oven for 10 minutes, so the butter and sugar melt together, then gently stir to give the nectarines a good basting of the buttery caramel. Return to the oven for a further 15–20 minutes.

Pour the custard over the fruit: some bits will float up, which is totally fine, and you'll also see a gorgeous marbled effect as the melted butter meets the batter. Reduce the oven temperature to 160°C fan/320°F/gas 4 and bake for 40–50 minutes until the custard has set and is caramelized. Leave to cool in the tray, then dust with icing (confectioners') sugar.

Allow to cool before eating. This will keep for 3 days in an airtight container in the fridge.

You can always double the batter recipe; it keeps for a few days in the fridge and makes pretty decent pancakes.

RASPBERRY & WHITE CHOCOLATE BAKEWELL

Don't be fooled by the name of this cake; it is merely a nod to the British Bakewell style, and actually has its roots in the rather fancy French friand, a small cake famed for its unusually dense yet somehow light and tender texture. Many years ago, we made them in our café, and somewhere along the line we decided to squeeze all that continental classiness into a traybake, so we bent it to our will and the result is a rather tasty Anglo-French slab of sustenance. Perfect for an end-of-summer picnic with a glass of something crisp and cold, or a flask of tea.

250g (9oz) soft butter
375g (13¼oz) caster
  (superfine) sugar
8 medium eggs
250g (9oz) ground almonds
210g (7½oz) plain
  (all-purpose) flour
1 teaspoon salt
200g (7oz) white chocolate chips
  (see notes)
250g (9oz) fresh raspberries
75g (2½oz) flaked almonds
icing (confectioners') sugar,
  for dusting

Preheat the oven to 180°C fan/350°F/gas 6 and line your 22 x 33 x 5cm (8½ x 13 x 2in) baking tray (sheet pan), see page 7.

Beat the softened butter and sugar together until combined and light in colour. Next, add the eggs and beat until fully combined and emulsified, then add the ground almonds, flour and salt. Mix until fully combined – there's no need to beat this furiously, just enough to create a nice smooth batter.

Add the white chocolate chips and raspberries to the mixing bowl and fold through so they're evenly dispersed. Keep mixing until ripples of pink raspberry juice begin to appear, but don't break up the raspberries too much, as you do want some bigger bursts of fruit.

Pour the mixture into your lined tray and spread it out evenly using a spatula. Finally, sprinkle the flaked almonds evenly across the top and place in the oven. Bake for 45–55 minutes. You're looking for a lovely light golden caramelization to the cake and the flaked almonds.

Leave to cool in the tray for at least 15 minutes, then remove from the tray and dust with icing (confectioners') sugar before serving while still a little warm. This will keep for 5 days in an airtight container in the fridge.

There's no reason why this recipe wouldn't work with blackberries or other soft fruits of the same ilk.

If you can't get hold of white chocolate chips, put white chocolate buttons in a food processor and blitz to create little shards: you want the pieces to be relatively small.

CARROT CAKE WITH CREAM CHEESE FROSTING

This recipe is a bit of a roller-coaster ride but absolutely worth it, so get strapped in for the best carrot cake of your life. The ingredients list may look a little daunting and there's a lot going on, but it's actually an easy cake to make, and when you taste it, there's balance in all the chaos. The acidity collides with the sweetness to create a firecracker of flavour, then the smoothness of the cream cheese contrasts perfectly with the crunch of walnuts and coconut.

TO MAKE THE CAKE

300ml (10fl oz) / (270g/9½oz)
  sunflower oil or rapeseed
  (canola) oil
350g (12oz) soft light brown sugar
4 medium eggs
100g (3½oz) ground almonds
100g (3½oz) walnut pieces
  (see note)
100g (3½oz) sultanas (golden
  raisins)
100g (3½oz) desiccated (dried
  shredded) coconut
250g (9oz) self-raising flour
2 tablespoons ground mixed
  (pumpkin pie) spice
1 teaspoon bicarbonate of soda
  (baking soda)
1 teaspoon salt
400g (14oz) grated carrots
finely grated zest and juice of
  1 orange
finely grated zest and juice of
  1 lemon

TO MAKE THE ICING

50g (1¾oz) soft butter
300g (10½oz) cream cheese
  (Philadelphia is pretty good
  for this)
juice of ½ lemon
50g (1¾oz) icing (confectioners')
  sugar

finely grated zest of 1 lime or
  some crushed walnuts, to finish
  (optional)

Preheat the oven to 160°C fan/320°F/gas 4 and line your 22 x 33 x 5cm (8½ x 13 x 2in) baking tray (sheet pan), see page 7.

To make the cake, combine the oil and sugar in a large mixing bowl, then add the eggs and mix until smooth. Stir in the ground almonds, walnuts, sultanas (golden raisins) and coconut. Sift in the flour, mixed (pumpkin pie) spice, bicarbonate of soda (baking soda) and salt, then fold in gently. Add the grated carrots, along with the zest and juice of the orange and lemon, then mix thoroughly, remembering to scrape down the sides of the bowl. Check the bottom of the mixing bowl, too, as the sugar and oil tend to play hide-and-seek down there.

When all the ingredients are well combined, pour into your lined baking tray and bake for 45–50 minutes. Test to see if the cake is cooked by sticking a knife in the middle; it should come out clean.

Transfer the cake to a wire rack or chopping board and leave to cool, now make the icing. Beat the butter in a stand mixer on a slow speed (or by hand), adding the cream cheese a dollop at a time, then add the lemon juice and keep mixing. Finally, sift in the icing (confectioners') sugar and mix well. When the cake has fully cooled, spread the icing evenly on top. Keep it simple or decorate with lime zest for a bit of funky colour and extra zing, or some crushed walnuts for added crunch.

This will keep for 5 days in an airtight container in the fridge.

You can try other kinds of icing here, like the Coconut Cream Icing (page 143), which would make it a dairy-free cake. Also, it's a little extra work, but lightly toasting the walnuts beforehand gives them better texture and flavour.

RASPBERRY CROISSANT CROWN CAKE

This isn't where we tell you to hand-make a load of croissants, or to go out and buy them fresh from your local artisan bakery. This recipe is designed to be made from the croissants that are a little stale and are going cheap or about to be binned, so it's a great way to reduce waste. An end-of-day supermarket dash for the yellow-label rush hour is your best bet for some reduced pastries. You can use almond croissants, pain au chocolat or Danishes with dried fruit, but none will work better than classic original butter croissants.

about 7 pastries (plain croissants
 are best)
5 medium eggs
390g (13¾oz) caster
 (superfine) sugar
80g (3oz) plain (all-purpose) flour
520ml (17½fl oz) double
 (heavy) cream
1 teaspoon vanilla extract
230g (8¼oz) raspberries
icing (confectioners') sugar,
 for dusting

NUT FREE

Preheat the oven to 180°C fan/350°F/gas 6 and line your 22 x 33 x 5cm (8½ x 13 x 2in) baking tray (sheet pan), see page 7.

Tear up your old pastries into strips, keeping them quite long and chunky. Lay them gently in the lined baking tray – don't press them down, as you want them to have a nice height so they stick out at jagged angles.

In a mixing bowl, beat the eggs and sugar until combined, then sift in the flour, a little at a time, mixing well with a whisk between each addition. Finally, pour in the cream and vanilla and mix until smooth.

Decant into a jug and pour this mixture delicately all around the torn croissants. Give the tray a little bang on the surface to get rid of any air bubbles that might be ensnared in the tangle of pastry, then scatter the raspberries evenly over the top.

Bake for around 50 minutes, or until the custard has risen and set slightly.

Leave to cool in the tray, then dust with icing (confectioners') sugar before serving.

Best eaten on the day it's made to retain the crunch, but it will keep for a couple of days in an airtight container in the fridge.

RHUBARB CRUMBLE CAKE

As far as we know, it's a crime to make a small crumble. You'd have to be a real piece of work to entertain the idea of making 'just enough', and most people get so enthusiastic when it comes to this pudding that they over-cater with wild abandon, leaving crumble on the menu for days afterwards. This recipe takes the crumble into sturdier territory, creating a movable feast that can be eaten anytime, anywhere, but is most likely to be scoffed hot with ice cream after your Sunday roast.

TO MAKE THE BASE
AND TOPPING

400g (14oz) plain
  (all-purpose) flour
200g (7oz) sugar
100g (3½oz) ground almonds
300g (10½oz) butter, cold
  and cubed
a pinch of salt
a splash of cold water (20–30ml/
  1½–2 tablespoons)
100g (3½oz) flaked almonds

TO MAKE THE FILLING

600g (1lb 5oz) forced rhubarb,
  chopped
200g (7oz) caster (superfine) sugar
1 teaspoon vanilla extract, or the
  seeds from 1 pod
finely grated zest and juice of
  1 orange

Preheat the oven to 160°C fan/320°F/gas 4 and line your 22 x 33 x 5cm (8½ x 13 x 2in) baking tray (sheet pan), see page 7.

For this cake, you make the base and topping together in one bowl. Start by adding all the ingredients, except the water and flaked almonds, to a large bowl. Rub together with your hands until you get a breadcrumb-like consistency. Then, remove half the mixture and place it in a separate bowl, mixing in the flaked almonds. Add a splash of cold water to the mixture still in the original bowl and work it into a pastry with your hands until it forms one large clump.

If you like to be precise with your baking, you can roll this out using a rolling pin and then place it in the lined tray, or you can just go for the more rustic approach and press it into the base of the tray with the palms of your hands. Whichever method you use, make sure you get a good even spread. Bake for 30 minutes, or until it begins to colour.

Meanwhile, make the filling by mixing together the rhubarb, sugar, vanilla and orange zest and juice in a heavy-based saucepan over a low heat. Let this stew, stirring occasionally, for 10–15 minutes until the rhubarb starts to relax and soften a little, then turn off the heat.

When the base has finished baking, it should be firm and slightly browned. Remove from the oven and top it with the stewed rhubarb, spreading it out evenly with a spatula. Sprinkle the reserved crumble and flaked almond mixture over the top. Increase the oven temperature to 170°C fan/340°F/gas 5 and bake for a further 35–40 minutes, or until the crumble topping starts to get a little colour.

Best served warm with cold custard, but you can always snack on a cold slice in the middle of the night, standing in your dressing gown.

This will keep for up to a week in an airtight container in the fridge.

This recipe will work with almost any soft fruit, although you might need to adjust the lemon and sugar quantities to balance the acidity and sweetness. Fill the crumble with peaches, plums and apricots, or the classic mix of apple and blackberry. Summer berries, gooseberries, pineapple or mango would also be a welcome change. Herbs like lemon thyme or rosemary can add depth.

PASSION FRUIT CHEESECAKE

The initial inspiration for this recipe came from a 2009 copy of *The Australian Women's Weekly Food* magazine. Australia has a trailblazing culture for modern baking, and nothing represents it better than this sun-soaked, mood-lifting banger. The passion fruit flavour is perfectly complemented by the coconut, and the brandy snap-style base brings texture, while the added lemon juice in the cheesecake mixture keeps the sweetness down and the freshness up.

TO MAKE THE BASE
125g (4¼oz) soft butter
250g (9oz) caster (superfine) sugar
1 medium egg
100g (3½oz) plain (all-purpose) flour
a pinch of salt

TO MAKE THE FILLING
375g (13¼oz) cream cheese
250g (9oz) caster sugar
6 medium eggs
½ teaspoon vanilla extract
80g (3oz) fresh passion fruit pulp (about 6 ripe passion fruits)
75ml (2½fl oz) fresh lemon juice (about 2 small lemons' worth)
100g (3½oz) plain flour
100g (3½oz) desiccated (dried shredded) coconut, plus extra for sprinkling
125ml (4¼fl oz) whole milk

TO MAKE THE SYRUP
1 tablespoon apricot jam
50ml (1¾fl oz) water

NUT FREE

Preheat the oven to 180°C fan/350°F/gas 6 and line your 22 x 33 x 5cm (8½ x 13 x 2in) baking tray (sheet pan), see page 7.

To make the base, beat together the butter and sugar in a large mixing bowl until well combined, then add the egg and mix together. Sift in the flour and salt and fold in until smooth. Spread into your lined tray using a spatula, making sure to get an even spread across the tray, right into the corners.

Bake for around 25 minutes, or until the base has a dark gold colour. It might rise up around the edges in places, but that's OK: it creates a really nice crispy edge and helps to hold the cheesecake mix in place.

Meanwhile, to make the cheesecake mixture, beat together the cream cheese and sugar in a large mixing bowl until smooth, then add the eggs and vanilla and beat gently until emulsified. Add the passion fruit pulp, along with the lemon juice, and combine well. Sift in the flour and fold in, then add the coconut. Once that's all combined, slowly pour in the milk and stir until you have a fully combined mixture.

Once your cooked base is out of the oven, pour the cheesecake mixture over the top and return to the oven for around 50 minutes, or until the top is set and slightly doming around the edges.

While the cheesecake is baking, make the syrup by mixing together the apricot jam and water in a small bowl. When the cheesecake comes out of the oven, brush the top with the syrup and sprinkle over a little desiccated (dried shredded) coconut: the syrup helps the coconut stick.

Leave to cool in the tray before transferring to a chopping board before serving.

Best eaten at room temperature or chilled. This will keep for 5 days in an airtight container in the fridge.

This feels more like a dessert than a slice of cake, so try serving with a little whipped cream and some more fresh passion fruit to elevate the state of affairs to middle-class stardom.

VANILLA CHEESECAKE

One of our bakers has a theory that to add anything other than the acidity of lemon or the bouquet of vanilla to a cheesecake would be to gild the lily: clearly, she is a purist, who is unmoved by all the chocolate, caramel and strawberry variations out there. Perhaps she is right, and this is as good as cheesecake gets. The base in this recipe is a baked pastry that holds up better than the usual broken-up biscuit (cookie) crumb foundation, which always feels a bit like building a house on sand. We like to make cake with good foundations.

TO MAKE THE BASE

125g (4¼oz) soft butter
250g (9oz) caster
  (superfine) sugar
1 medium egg
100g (3½oz) plain
  (all-purpose) flour
a pinch of salt

TO MAKE THE FILLING

680g (1lb 8oz) cream cheese
  (use supermarket own-brand)
185g (6½oz) caster sugar
6 medium eggs
20ml (1½ tablespoons) vanilla
  extract
75ml (2½fl oz) lemon juice
60g (2oz) plain flour
210ml (7fl oz) whole milk

NUT FREE

Preheat the oven to 180°C fan/350°F/gas 6 and line your 22 x 33 x 5cm (8½ x 13 x 2in) baking tray (sheet pan), see page 7.

To make the base, beat together the butter and caster (superfine) sugar in a large mixing bowl, then add the egg and give it another good beating. Sift in the flour and salt and fold in until smooth. Spread into your lined tray using a spatula, making sure to get an even spread across the tray, right into the corners. Bake for around 25 minutes, or until the base has a dark gold colour. It might rise up around the edges, but that's OK: this will help to cradle the cheesecake mix.

Now make the filling. In a large bowl, mix together the cream cheese and sugar, then add the eggs and whip gently until you have a nicely emulsified mixture. Pour in the vanilla and lemon juice and mix together, then sift in half the flour and fold it in. Sift in the remaining flour and fold together until you have a smooth, lump-free mixture, then slowly pour in the milk and stir to combine. Remove the base from the oven and pour the cream cheese mix over the top. Return to the oven and bake for a further 35 minutes, or until you have a smooth, set top.

Best eaten at room temperature or chilled. This will keep for 5 days in an airtight container in the fridge.

This is one of those cakes that, when eaten chilled, has the kind of texture that makes it feel like you're eating something refreshing - it's light and summery rather than heavy. If you're inclined to add fruit to this recipe, please don't add it before baking: simply serve the cheesecake with fresh fruit.

GINGER DICK

We've chosen this name to provoke the mind and conjure the classic British dessert, as there's something distinctly puddingy about this cake. Aside from the name though, there's little resemblance to its distant cousin of the spotted variety. This is more closely related to shop-bought Jamaican gingerbread, but with added texture from the golden nuggets of crystallized ginger. It keeps well and is delicious cold, but it would make no sense if you went to the trouble of making it without trying it hot with custard at least once.

TO MAKE THE CAKE
180g (6¼oz) dried dates, chopped
80ml (2¾fl oz) boiling water
360g (12¾oz) butter
280g (9¾oz) black treacle (molasses)
180g (6¼oz) soft light brown sugar
2 medium eggs
360g (12¾oz) self-raising flour
1 teaspoon salt
½ teaspoon ground ginger
¼ teaspoon ground cinnamon
¼ teaspoon ground cardamom
180g (6¼oz) crystallized ginger (see note)

TO MAKE THE TOPPING
60–70g (2–2½oz) black treacle
150g (5¼oz) crystallized ginger, cut into small pieces

NUT FREE

Preheat the oven to 160°C fan/320°F/gas 4 and line your 22 x 33 x 5cm (8½ x 13 x 2in) baking tray (sheet pan), see page 7.

Get started by covering the dates with the boiling water, and setting them aside to soak, ideally for about 10 minutes or so.

Meanwhile, melt the butter, treacle and sugar in a heavy-based saucepan over a medium heat, stirring until the sugar is dissolved, then transfer to the bowl of your stand mixer, or a large mixing bowl, and mix slowly. Add the eggs and the soaked dates, including the soaking water, increasing your speed until everything comes together and emulsifies. Sift the flour, salt and spices into a separate bowl, then slowly add all the dry ingredients to the mixture, along with the crystalized ginger. Mix it all together, then pour into your lined tray and bake for 50 minutes.

Make the topping by reusing your pan from earlier to gently warm the treacle over a low heat. When the cake comes out of the oven, carefully remove from the tray and place on a chopping board. Brush the treacle on to the cake using a pastry brush and then scatter the crystallized ginger nuggets over the sticky surface.

Best eaten still warm or cooled. This will keep for a week in an airtight container in the fridge.

Some crystallized ginger comes in bigger nuggets than others, so you might want to chop them further if they seem out of proportion to the cake. The type we use comes in cubes of about 3-5mm (⅛-¼in).

SESAME, ORANGE & FIG SLICE

Using seasonal, non-imported figs for this recipe can leave you with a relatively small window of availability. So, if you're in a sticky situation fig-wise, and can't find the fresh ones, try cutting up some dried figs and putting them in the mix, then dollop a few spoonfuls of fig jam on top. While the figs turn on the charm with some super-squidgy sweetness, the sesame adds an element of savoury complexity.

200g (7oz) caster (superfine) sugar
200g (7oz) soft brown sugar
200g (7oz) soft butter
3 medium eggs
finely grated zest and juice of
  1 orange
250g (9oz) toasted sesame seeds
300g (10½oz) plain
  (all-purpose) flour
1 teaspoon baking powder
½ teaspoon salt
8–10 whole ripe figs, quartered
  lengthways

Preheat the oven to 160°C fan/320°F/gas 4 and line your 22 x 33 x 5cm (8½ x 13 x 2in) baking tray (sheet pan), see page 7.

Start by combining your caster (superfine) sugar, brown sugar and butter in a stand mixer, or a large mixing bowl, and beat until fluffy. Now add your eggs, one at a time, and beat until everything is well combined. Next, stir in the orange zest and juice, followed by 200g (7oz) of the sesame seeds.

Fold in the flour, baking powder and salt until combined, then transfer the mixture to your baking tray, spreading it into the corners and levelling it out using a spatula. Sprinkle over the remaining 50g (1¾oz) of sesame seeds. Finally, press the figs on to the top of the cake, then bake for 40 minutes until the top becomes darker and the figs are nice and jammy. Remove from the oven and cool on a wire rack or chopping board.

Best eaten still warm or cooled. This will keep for 4 days in an airtight container in the fridge.

WHITE CHOCOLATE, MISO & CINNAMON COOKIE SLICE

This is similar to a blondie: heavy on the richness, and dense and gooey as you like. The miso brings a different balance to the flavour, working in tandem with the white chocolate to give you a hit of savoury with your sweetness, while the hazelnuts add welcome texture.

100g (3½oz) whole hazelnuts
250g (9oz) soft butter
300g (10½oz) soft light
  brown sugar
1 teaspoon miso paste or salt
3 medium eggs
130g (4½oz) black treacle
  (molasses)
450g (1lb) plain (all-purpose) flour
1 tablespoon bicarbonate of soda
  (baking soda)
2 teaspoons ground cinnamon
2 teaspoons ground ginger
1½ teaspoons ground mixed
  (pumpkin pie) spice
250g (9oz) white chocolate chips

Turn on the oven to 170°C fan/340°F/gas 5 and line your 22 x 33 x 5cm (8½ x 13 x 2in) baking tray (sheet pan), see page 7.

While the oven is still warming up, pop the hazelnuts on the lined tray and place in the oven for 10–15 minutes, then remove them and transfer them to one half of a clean dish towel. Fold the other half of the dish towel over the top and rub the nuts through the towel with the palms of your hands: this will remove the hazelnut skins. Leave to cool slightly, then discard all the skins. Smash the nuts up, either in a food processor or by wrapping them back up in the towel and beating with a rolling pin, then set them aside for later.

Heat the butter in a heavy-based saucepan over a low heat for a few minutes until it melts and starts turning a golden-brown colour. Then transfer the hot butter to the bowl of your stand mixer, or a large mixing bowl, and add the sugar, mixing on a high speed (or by hand) for a few minutes until it cools and bonds together. Add the miso and eggs and mix until it forms a glossy emulsion. Next add the treacle and all the dry ingredients, along with the white chocolate chips. Mix on a medium speed until fully combined. Scrape down the sides of the bowl and around the bottom to stop a mosh pit of ingredients gathering down there, and give it a final mix. Turn the mixture out into the lined tray and press it down evenly.

Bake for 35–40 minutes for that really soft cookie style, or for a little longer if you want crunchy edges. Remove from the tray and, while the cake is still warm, use a knife to mark out the portions before things firm up. If you want a gooey centre, sit the tray in some icy water as soon as the cake comes out of the oven, or put it straight into the freezer for 20 minutes. This will halt the cooking from the residual heat, meaning the middle stays a little undercooked.

Best eaten still warm or cooled. This will keep for a week in an airtight container in the fridge.

Try using different types of miso paste. Barley, rice and soy bean miso all have different flavours. They can be dark, pale or red in colour, but all carry that kick of umami.

CHOCOLATE CHIP COOKIE CAKE

Getting a milk moustache from drinking an icy cold glass of creaminess becomes even more nostalgic when paired with a chocolate-laden cookie. This basic recipe should be your first step towards becoming some kind of cookie monster; it cuts out the faff of chilling your dough in the fridge so you can bake it straight after mixing. As always, you can flavour the cookies in your own way: peanut butter, crystallized ginger, ground cinnamon, cocoa powder, any kind of nut or seeds, or maybe a scattering of oats for texture.

250g (9oz) soft butter
200g (7oz) soft light brown sugar
250g (9oz) caster
 (superfine) sugar
2 medium eggs
400g (14oz) chocolate chips
 (milk or dark)
450g (1lb) self-raising flour
a pinch of sea salt

TO MAKE THE TOPPING
30g (1oz) melted chocolate
 (milk or dark)
a pinch of sea salt flakes (optional)

NUT FREE

Pictured on page 42.

Preheat the oven to 160°C fan/320°F/gas 4 and line your 22 x 33 x 5cm (8½ x 13 x 2in) baking tray (sheet pan), see page 7.

Melt the butter in a pan over a low heat, then transfer it to the bowl of your stand mixer or a large mixing bowl, along with both types of sugar, and cream together until smooth. Add the eggs one at a time, while still mixing, and beat until everything is combined and the mixture is a bit fluffy.

Add the chocolate chips and sift in the flour, along with a pinch of salt. Mix with a hook attachment until it forms a dough, or use your hands to bring it all together. Using a spatula or your hands, press the cookie dough into your lined tray.

Bake for 40–45 minutes if you want a really soft cookie, or for a little longer if you want crunchy edges. It's OK for it to have a little wobble in the middle.

To decorate, flick the melted chocolate across the top of the cake with a fork: try to bring out your inner artist and go a bit wild with this. If you want the cookie slices to have a touch of sophistication, you can sprinkle a pinch of sea salt flakes on top.

Best eaten still warm or cooled. This will keep for a week in an airtight container in the fridge.

Using an alternative to self-raising flour, such as wholemeal (wholewheat) or a touch of rye, will bring a maltiness and a slight change in texture. Just be sure to add some baking powder: a teaspoon or two should give sufficient lift.

If you don't have chocolate chips, wrap up a chocolate bar in a dish towel and smash it into little pieces.

PEANUT BUTTER CUP TIFFIN

You might recall that E.T. was a massive Reece's Pieces fan, which goes to show the universal appeal of peanut and chocolate, with the combination reaching far beyond this world. We reckon little old E.T. would love this one too, as it's a take on the iconic snack, albeit a bit purer on the ingredients front. It's still very rich, though, so you may need to micro-dose to get your hit, as a full slice could bring on gout. The recipe also works with tahini for a sesame version if you fancy switching out the peanuts. This keeps for an age, but the puffed rice may get a little chewy.

TO MAKE THE PEANUT BUTTER PASTE

200g (7oz) wholemeal digestive biscuits (graham crackers), we use Doves
200g (7oz) peanut butter (crunchy or smooth)
100g (3½oz) icing (confectioners') sugar
a pinch of salt

TO MAKE THE BASE

300g (10½oz) dark chocolate, broken into pieces
150g (5¼oz) butter
3 tablespoons golden syrup
100g (3½oz) puffed rice

TO MAKE THE TOPPING

300g (10½oz) dark chocolate, broken into small pieces
50g (1¾oz) butter
1 tablespoon golden syrup
50g (1¾oz) peanut butter, crunchy or smooth

Pictured on page 42.

First, line your 22 x 33 x 5cm (8½ x 13 x 2in) baking tray (sheet pan), see page 7.

Make your peanut butter paste by blitzing the biscuits (graham crackers) in a food processor until they form a powder. Then add the peanut butter, icing (confectioners') sugar and salt, blitzing between additions. Go easy as you add the icing sugar, otherwise you could be engulfed in sweet sugar clouds.

Plonk spoonfuls of the peanut butter paste into your lined tray, creating boulders evenly dotted over the base of the tray.

Next, make the base layer by melting the chocolate, butter and golden syrup together in a bain-marie (see page 8). Remove from the heat when you have a happy bowl of melted ingredients, then add the puffed rice and fold through with a spatula. Pour this over the little boulders of peanut butter paste; it will settle and level out by itself so the boulders are just peeking through.

To make the topping, scrape the bowl clean, then return it to the bain-marie and add the chocolate, butter and golden syrup. While these are melting, send the base layer somewhere cold to toughen up: the freezer is best for this. Once melted and combined, pour the topping over the chilled base, then dot teaspoons of peanut butter across the top. Use a pointy object (like a toothpick or skewer) to swirl the peanut butter into the chocolate topping in whatever design you like. Return the cake to the fridge for a couple of hours before removing and slicing.

Best eaten chilled. This will keep for at least 2 weeks in an airtight container in the fridge.

You can skip the peanut butter paste if you want to and just mix broken biscuit (cookie) pieces, dried fruit and various nuts into the chocolate base layer. Marshmallows can add a sponginess against all that crunch and take you into rocky road territory.

BROWNIES

Brownies are a real speciality at The Exploding Bakery. The recipes in this section are the fruits of a brownie obsession that started many years ago as a reaction to some of the margarine and preservative-addled imitations available out there. We vowed never to make a bad brownie, to dial the quality up to 11 and flip the 'V's to the mass-produced rubbish. We believe brownies should be fudgy and rich; that they should taste of the chocolate and not the sugar; that they should always make you happy; and that they can cure even the biggest of sulks.

A hot brownie, fresh from the oven and served up with cream, is arguably the best dessert in the world: five simple ingredients punching above their weight. Choosing a high-quality chocolate brings all sorts of complex flavours to the table. Real butter enhances that, and with a variety of flours and nut flours to choose from, you can change the texture to suit your desires. Some of you may be inclined to stuff Jammie Dodgers or rainbow-coloured sweets (candies) all over your bakes, but we feel you'd be doing them an injustice, and should instead allow the brownie to stand up on its own two feet with the integrity and dignity it deserves. Save the biscuits (cookies) for dunking, keep the Smarties and M&M's for the car, and roll out the red carpet for the pure brownie A-listers.

Top tip: once you've poured your brownie batter into the baking tray (sheet pan), it's always a good idea to give the tray a good bang on the worktop: this will release any trapped air bubbles in the mixture. If left unchecked, these can expand in the oven and form pockets under the brownie.

STRAIGHT-UP BROWNIE

To make a great brownie, you only need five simple ingredients: chocolate, butter, eggs, sugar and flour. For many, simple is best. This is our classic brownie: it's straight-up, no bullshit – ideal for the chocolate purists. Perfectly gooey in the centre when warm from the oven, then slowly develops a slightly crispy exterior. We'd always recommend holding your nerve and taking a brownie out of the oven while it still jiggles, but you can bake it a little longer if you like a more cake-like texture.

420g (14¾oz) dark chocolate,
  broken into pieces
300g (10½oz) butter
375g (13¼oz) caster
  (superfine) sugar
6 medium eggs
250g (9oz) plain (all-purpose) flour
1 tablespoon cocoa powder
1 teaspoon salt

NUT FREE

Preheat the oven to 150°C fan/300°F/gas 3½ and line your 22 x 33 x 5cm (8½ x 13 x 2in) baking tray (sheet pan), see page 7.

Melt the chocolate and butter together in a bain-marie (see page 8), or if you prefer, you can do this in a heavy-based saucepan over a very low heat. Once melted, transfer to a large mixing bowl or the bowl of your stand mixer and start adding the sugar, a little at a time, while mixing, until the sugar dissolves.

Add the eggs and beat on a high speed until the mixture becomes smooth and glossy and starts to pull away from the sides of the bowl without sticking to it. That's how you know everything has emulsified. If using a mixer, it will also make a different sound, moving from a slapping to a thudding noise: this means things have thickened slightly.

Gradually add the plain (all-purpose) flour, cocoa powder and salt, adding a bit at a time to stop the cocoa billowing out. Scrape down the sides of the bowl with a spatula then give it another light mix to make sure everything is fully combined.

Pour the mixture into your lined tray and bake for 30–35 minutes. You need the brownie to be slightly undercooked to get that truffley, fudgy texture, so it should have a wobble when it comes out of the oven: the truffle shuffle!

Leave to cool for at least 15 minutes in the tray before transferring to a chopping board and cutting – or, if you fancy it, you can spoon out portions from the tray while it's still warm and serve with ice cream.

Best eaten while still warm in the middle. This will keep for a week when stored in an airtight container in the fridge.

Brownie ice-cream sandwiches anyone? As this brownie has brawn, we'd recommend it as the brownie of choice for this snack. Let a piece of brownie chill, then slice it lengthways and spread a generous layer of soft ice cream on one side before squishing the two halves back together.

KILLER VEGAN BROWNIE

The neutral flavours of the oil and oats really allow the chocolate to sing in this cake, but feel free to try it with a peppery olive oil or a grassy cold-pressed rapeseed (canola). This is a solid stand-alone recipe, which also works well as the foundation for your own creations.

425g (15oz) dark chocolate,
  broken into pieces
190ml (7fl oz) / (170g/6½oz)
  rapeseed (canola) oil
330g (11¾oz) caster
  (superfine) sugar
25g (1oz) cornflour (cornstarch)
40ml (1½fl oz) cold water
260ml (9¾fl oz) boiling water
175g (4¼oz) ground almonds
125g (4¼oz) oat flour (gluten-free)
50g (1¾oz) cocoa powder
1 teaspoon salt

VEGAN
GLUTEN FREE

Preheat the oven to 160°C fan/320°F/gas 4 and line your 22 x 33 x 5cm (8½ x 13 x 2in) baking tray (sheet pan), see page 7.

Melt the chocolate and oil in a bain-marie (see page 8) until combined, then transfer to a large mixing bowl or the bowl of your stand mixer, but leave the bain-marie on the heat with the water in the pan still simmering. Add the sugar to the chocolate and oil mixture and combine.

In the same bowl you used for the bain-marie, mix together the cornflour (cornstarch) and cold water. Once they're combined, add the boiling water, then place the bowl back on the simmering pan to heat up as you stir. The cornflour will thicken the mixture to a dropping consistency. When that happens, you can transfer this mixture to your bowl and beat until the batter becomes glossy and emulsified. Then slowly add the remaining dry ingredients, mixing until fully combined. If the mixture splits, add a splash of boiling water to bring it together. Pour into your lined tray and bake for 40–45 minutes until just set.

Best eaten while still a little warm. This will keep for a week in an airtight container in the fridge.

Out of the three main base recipes, this one is the firmest, so bear this in mind when you're plotting alterations. If you're in the mood to experiment, the liquid in the cornflour paste can easily be switched out for something crazy like a stout or red wine.

PEANUT BUTTER BROWNIE

We've tried a few different peanut butters for this, and found the ones that work best are about 95 per cent peanuts, with a bit of oil and salt. We use the smooth kind, but if you're a crunchy kind of person, then give it a go. For the candied nuts, we really love the look of peanuts with their red skin still on. The cloying nature of nut butters needs to be embraced, but if it's all a bit too much, reduce the amount of peanut butter and use a little jam: you could even stir some broken-up banana chips through the mixture for texture.

TO MAKE THE CANDIED PEANUTS

100g (3½oz) red-skin peanuts
1 tablespoon golden syrup
a pinch of salt

TO MAKE THE BROWNIE

370g (13oz) dark chocolate,
    broken into pieces
150ml (5fl oz) / (135g/4¾oz)
    rapeseed (canola) oil
285g (10oz) caster
    (superfine) sugar
20g (¾oz) cornflour (cornstarch)
35ml (1¼fl oz) cold water
185ml (6¼fl oz) boiling water
150g (5¼oz) ground almonds
100g (3½oz) oat flour (gluten-free)
40g (1½oz) cocoa powder
1 teaspoon salt
150g (5¼oz) smooth peanut butter

A piping bag is useful for this
    recipe, but is not essential

VEGAN
GLUTEN FREE

Turn on the oven to 160°C fan/320°F/gas 4 and line your 22 x 33 x 5cm (8½ x 13 x 2in) baking tray (sheet pan), as well as a baking sheet, see page 7.

To make the candied peanuts, put the peanuts on the lined baking sheet with the golden syrup and a pinch of salt. Pop in the oven while it's heating up. After 10 minutes, give them a stir with a spatula, then return to the oven and cook for a further 10 minutes, or until the golden syrup starts to become really sticky and darkens in colour. Once done, take out of the oven (but leave the oven on) and separate out the peanuts so they aren't all clumped together. Set aside to cool.

Meanwhile, melt the chocolate in a bain-marie (see page 8), then add the oil and leave to warm and merge evenly. Pour into a large mixing bowl or the bowl of your stand mixer, but leave the bain-marie on the heat with the water in the pan still simmering. Add the sugar to the chocolate and oil mixture and combine.

In the same bowl you used for the bain-marie, mix together the cornflour (cornstarch) and cold water. Once they're combined, add the boiling water, then place the bowl back on the simmering pan to heat up as you stir. The mixture will thicken. Add this cornflour mixture to the chocolate and sugar bowl and mix until glossy and fully emulsified. If the mixture splits, add a splash of boiling water to bring it together. Now add the ground almonds, oat flour, cocoa powder and salt, then mix to combine.

Pour the mixture into the other lined tray and spread to the corners so it's level. Fill the piping bag with the peanut butter and snip a 5mm (¼in) hole in the end. Use it to pipe patterns of your fancy across the brownie. If you don't have a piping bag, just dollop the peanut butter on top. You can swirl it in with a toothpick to make pretty patterns. Sprinkle the candied peanuts over the top and bake for 40–45 minutes. You'll know it's ready when the top becomes firm, but the brownie still has a little jiggle in it.

Best eaten once cooled. This will keep for a week in an airtight container in the fridge.

Try replacing the salt in the brownie mixture with a teaspoon of Marmite. You can melt this into the boiling water. The flavour really plays off the peanut butter.

ALMOND BROWNIE

Our almond brownie is the bedrock of our company: it's the foundation on which we built our house of cake over 10 years ago, and remains one of the best-selling cakes we've ever produced. Because of the simplicity of a brownie, it's so important to get the ingredients right. Variables outside your control will always affect the final result – the moisture content of the butter you use, the acidity of the chocolate you choose or the accuracy of your oven – but if you start with the good stuff, at least you'll always know it's going to have banging flavour. So find yourself some single-origin chocolate, some real butter and high-quality free-range eggs, and get stuck in.

375g (13¼oz) dark chocolate,
  broken into pieces
375g (13¼oz) butter
300g (10½oz) caster
  (superfine) sugar
6 medium eggs
225g (8oz) ground almonds
1 teaspoon salt

GLUTEN FREE

Preheat the oven to 170°C fan/340°F/gas 5 and line your 22 x 33 x 5cm (8½ x 13 x 2in) baking tray (sheet pan), see page 7.

Melt the chocolate and butter together in a bain-marie (see page 8), stirring occasionally until they are combined and silky smooth. Pour the melted chocolate and butter into a large mixing bowl or the bowl of your stand mixer, then add the sugar and give it a quick mix, letting the sugar dissolve a little. Now add the eggs and beat until the mixture emulsifies.

Finally, fold in the ground almonds and salt until fully combined, then pour the batter into your lined tray. Bake for 25–30 minutes. The brownie should be just cooked when you take it out, with a little wobble in the middle.

Serve hot with ice cream or cool with lashings of cream.

Best eaten still warm in the middle. This will keep for up to 2 weeks in an airtight container in the fridge.

This can be made with hazelnut flour instead of ground almonds; it's pretty much a straight swap, assuming that the coarseness of the milled ingredients is the same. You could try out some other nut flours too.

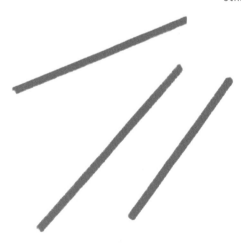

HALVA BROWNIE

Chocolate and sesame are a killer combo, and the bright green pistachios cleaved into the face of each slice of this brownie give an explosion of colour against the dark chocolate. The halva recipe can be adapted by using some rose water or orange blossom water, or adding some additional nuts. Obviously, popping to the shop to buy some halva is totally fine, but we think it's worth giving our vegan recipe a go.

TO MAKE THE HALVA
125g (4¼oz) caster
  (superfine) sugar
40g (1½oz) water
100g (3½oz) light tahini
40g (1½oz) shelled pistachios

TO MAKE THE BROWNIE
380g (13½oz) dark chocolate
150ml (5fl oz) / (135g/4¾oz)
  rapeseed (canola) oil
285g (10oz) caster sugar
20g (¾oz) cornflour (cornstarch)
35ml (1¼fl oz) cold water
185ml (6¼fl oz) boiling water
150g (5¼oz) ground almonds
100g (3½oz) oat flour (gluten-free)
40g (1½oz) cocoa powder
100g (3½oz) shelled pistachios
1 teaspoon salt
100g (3½oz) tahini

VEGAN
GLUTEN FREE

Pictured on page 53.

Preheat the oven to 160°C fan/320°F/gas 4 and line your 22 x 33 x 5cm (8½ x 13 x 2in) baking tray (sheet pan), see page 7.

To make the halva, you do need some Jedi instincts, as a lot depends on how thick the tahini is. It's best to stick with the same brand each time you make it to reduce the variables. Start by putting the sugar and water in a heavy-based saucepan over a medium heat. Bring to the boil and let it simmer for about 5 minutes (ideally, you want the temperature to reach 118°C/244°F), then pop the bottom of the pan into some cold water to cool things down a little.

Warm up the light tahini in a bain-marie (see page 8) and give it a good mix, then add the pistachios and stir with a spatula to combine. Stir the sugar syrup into the bowl of warm tahini while still on the bain-marie, adding a little at a time. Don't over-mix, or it'll become crumbly. The mixture will instantly become thick and turn into halva. Transfer the halva on to a sheet of baking parchment and leave to cool and set firm. You can cut it with a knife to make nice chunky bits for topping the brownie.

To make the brownie, melt the chocolate in a bain-marie, then add the oil and leave to warm and merge evenly. Pour into a large mixing bowl or the bowl of your stand mixer, but leave the bain-marie on the heat with the water in the pan still simmering. Add the sugar to the chocolate and oil and combine.

In the same bowl you used for the bain-marie, mix together the cornflour (cornstarch) and cold water. Once they're combined, add the boiling water, then place the bowl back on the simmering pan to heat up as you stir. The mixture will thicken. Add this cornflour mixture to the chocolate and sugar and mix until glossy and fully emulsified. If the mixture splits, add a splash of boiling water to bring it together. Now add the ground almonds, oat flour, cocoa powder, pistachios and salt, then mix to combine.

Pour the mixture into your lined tray and spread it out to the corners, making sure it's level.

Sprinkle all the chunks of halva over the top, pushing some down into the mix, then drizzle over the tahini in a random fashion. You can use a toothpick to create swirly shapes and psychedelic patterns. Bake for 30–40 minutes. You'll know it's ready when the top becomes firm and the halva has darkened a little, but the brownie still has a little jiggle in it.

Best eaten cool. This will keep for a week in an airtight container in the fridge.

COFFEE & WALNUT BROWNIE

It's not the usual way to make a coffee and walnut cake, but here we infuse finely ground espresso into the cake, grounds and all. The fine grind makes for an unusual texture that lets you know you've got some real coffee in there, as opposed to using the instant coffee or chicory extract methods. If the thought of coffee grinds in your gums puts you off, then you can just use the filtered coffee. The flavours here are immense, with sweet caramelized walnuts wrestling with the smoky coffee to the bitter end of every mouthful.

TO MAKE THE CANDIED NUTS
150g (5¼oz) walnuts
1 tablespoon golden syrup
a pinch of ground cardamom
a pinch of salt

TO MAKE THE COFFEE
60g (2oz) extra-fine ground coffee
130ml (4½fl oz) boiling water

TO MAKE THE BROWNIE
400g (14oz) dark chocolate,
  broken into pieces
150ml (5fl oz) / (135g/4¾oz)
  rapeseed (canola) oil
300g (10½oz) caster
  (superfine) sugar
20g (¾oz) cornflour (cornstarch)
35ml (1¼fl oz) cold water
175ml (6floz) boiling water
140g (5oz) ground almonds
100g (3½oz) oat flour (gluten-free)
40g (1½oz) cocoa powder
1 teaspoon salt

VEGAN
GLUTEN FREE

Pictured on page 53.

Preheat the oven to 150°C fan/300°F/gas 3½ and line your 22 x 33 x 5cm (8½ x 13 x 2in) baking tray (sheet pan), as well as a baking sheet, see page 7.

To make the candied nuts, put the walnuts on the lined baking sheet and drizzle with the golden syrup. Sprinkle with the ground cardamom and salt and bake for 10–15 minutes until toasty and glistening: check after 10 minutes, and turn them over with a spatula. Remove from the oven (but leave the oven on) and set aside to cool.

To make the coffee, put the ground coffee into a mug and add the boiling water. Set aside to infuse for a few minutes.

Meanwhile, melt the chocolate in a bain-marie (see page 8), then add the oil and leave to warm and merge evenly. Pour into a large mixing bowl or the bowl of your stand mixer, but leave the bain-marie on the heat with the water in the pan still simmering. Add the sugar to the chocolate and oil and combine.

In the same bowl you used for the bain-marie, mix together the cornflour (cornstarch) and cold water. Once they're combined, add the boiling water, then place the bowl back on the simmering pan to heat up as you stir. The mixture will thicken. Add this cornflour mixture to the chocolate and sugar and mix until glossy and fully emulsified. If the mixture splits, add a splash of boiling water to bring it together. Now add the ground almonds, oat flour, cocoa powder and salt, then pour in the mug of coffee and grounds. Mix to combine.

Pour the batter into the second lined tray and sprinkle the candied walnuts on top. Bake for 35–40 minutes. You'll know it's ready when the top becomes firm, but the brownie still has a little jiggle in it.

Best eaten cool. This will keep for 5 days in an airtight container in the fridge.

Of course, if you don't have real coffee then you can try this with instant. It's strangely a more familiar coffee flavour in cakes over the real stuff, as we've become institutionalized to that ingredient in baking.

FRUIT & NUT BROWNIE

The beauty of a vegan and gluten-free brownie is that it allows the chocolate to really shine, bringing the complex acidity centre stage. There's something about it that's remarkably similar to the experience of eating a Cadbury's Fruit & Nut bar, as the hazelnuts crunch between your teeth and the tea-soaked raisins get all up in your gums. The only difference is the chocolate flavour is in your face with a big smile, waving at you and saying hello. You'll probably say hello back.

TO MAKE THE CANDIED NUTS

100g (3½oz) blanched hazelnuts
100g (3½oz) flaked almonds
1 tablespoon golden syrup

TO MAKE THE BROWNIE

1 Earl Grey tea bag
125g (4¼oz) raisins
185ml (6¼fl oz) boiling water
35ml (1¼fl oz) cold water
20g (¾oz) cornflour (cornstarch)
360g (12¾oz) dark chocolate,
   broken into pieces
150ml (5fl oz) / (135g/4¾oz)
   rapeseed (canola) oil
285g (10oz) caster
   (superfine) sugar
150g (5¼oz) ground almonds
100g (3½oz) oat flour (gluten-free)
40g (1½oz) cocoa powder
50g (1¾oz) shelled pistachios
1 teaspoon salt

VEGAN
GLUTEN FREE

Preheat the oven to 150°C fan/300°F/gas 3½ and line your 22 x 33 x 5cm (8½ x 13 x 2in) baking tray (sheet pan), as well as a baking sheet, see page 7.

To make the candied nuts, put the hazelnuts and almonds on the lined baking sheet and drizzle with the golden syrup. Bake for 10 minutes, then check them to see how they're getting on. Turn them over with a spatula, then bake for another 5 minutes. Remove from the oven (but leave the oven on) and set aside to cool.

To make the brownie, put the tea bag and raisins in a bowl, then pour over the boiling water. Leave to infuse for a few minutes, then remove the bag. In a small bowl or mug, mix together the cold water and cornflour (cornstarch) to form a paste, then pour this into the bowl with the tea-soaked raisins and stir until it all thickens up. If it doesn't thicken, you may need to apply some heat to help the process; you can do this using a bain-marie (see page 8) or in short blasts using a microwave.

Next, melt the chocolate in a bain-marie, then add the oil and leave to warm and merge evenly. Pour into a large mixing bowl or the bowl of your stand mixer, then add the sugar. Mix to combine, then add the raisin and cornflour mixture and mix on a high speed (or by hand) until glossy and fully emulsified. If the mixture splits, add a splash of boiling water to bring it together. Add the ground almonds, oat flour, cocoa powder, pistachios and salt, and mix again to combine.

Pour the batter into the second lined tray and sprinkle the candied nuts on top. Bake for 35–40 minutes. You'll know it's ready when the top becomes firm, but the brownie still has a little jiggle in it.

Best eaten cool. This will keep for a week when stored in an airtight container in the fridge.

The combination of fruit and nut is a chewy, crunchy experience. Keep this in mind if you want to swap stuff out. A glass of Pedro Ximenez makes a handsome accompaniment.

CHERRY BROWNIE

When we first heard about pink ruby chocolate, it made us feel a little nauseous, and reminded us of all those ghastly fondant icings we were once so opposed to. But after a little education, we realized it's not a contrived colouring: it's a naturally pink and fruity chocolate. We thought it was a fun way to add some colour to a brownie and ricochet off the cherry bomb of flavour.

TO MAKE THE BROWNIE

200g (7oz) fresh cherries, pitted and chopped
1 heaped tablespoon cornflour (cornstarch)
350g (12oz) dark chocolate, broken into small pieces
350g (12oz) butter
280g (9¾oz) caster (superfine) sugar
5 medium eggs
300g (10½oz) ground almonds
1 teaspoon cocoa powder
1 teaspoon salt

TO MAKE THE TOPPING

180g (6¼oz) ruby chocolate
150g (5¼oz) whole fresh cherries, pitted, or 25g (1oz) freeze-dried
5g (¼oz) pink peppercorns

GLUTEN FREE

Preheat the oven to 160°C fan/320°F/gas 4 and line your 22 x 33 x 5cm (8½ x 13 x 2in) baking tray (sheet pan), see page 7

To make the brownie, place the chopped cherries in a bowl with the cornflour (cornstarch) and stir to coat. This will help to thicken their juices when cooking. Set aside.

Melt the chocolate and butter together in a bain-marie (see page 8). Once melted, pour into a large mixing bowl or the bowl of your stand mixer and add the sugar. Mix for a short while to allow the sugar to dissolve a little. Scrape down the sides of the bowl, then beat in the eggs until the mixture becomes smooth, glossy and emulsified. Add the ground almonds, cocoa powder and salt and mix until fully combined, then gently fold in the chopped cherries.

Transfer the mixture to your lined tray and bake for 35–40 minutes until the brownie is just set, but still has a little wobble in the middle. Leave to cool in the tray.

Once the brownie has cooled, you can make the tempered pink chocolate topping. Melt two thirds of the ruby chocolate in a bain-marie, stirring constantly. As soon as it's melted, remove the bowl from the heat and add the remaining ruby chocolate to the bowl and stir to melt. Scatter the cherries directly over the top of the brownie, then use a fork to quickly drizzle thin lines of the melted ruby chocolate over the top. Before the chocolate sets, sprinkle over the pink peppercorns.

Best eaten cool. This will keep for 4 days when stored in an airtight container in the fridge.

Ruby chocolate is expensive and can be a little hard to find. White chocolate will look great and still taste good with the cherry flavour.

RASPBERRY BROWNIE

This is a challenging recipe, but once you master making the *pâtes de fruits*, you can swap out the raspberries for lots of different fruits. Please get high-methoxyl yellow pectin, otherwise your fruit jelly will melt into the brownie when it cooks.

TO MAKE THE PÂTES DE FRUITS
150g (5¼oz) raspberries
110g (3¾oz) caster
  (superfine) sugar
3g high-methoxyl yellow pectin
  (non-reversible)
30g (1oz) glucose syrup
1g (¼ teaspoon) citric acid
½ teaspoon water

TO MAKE THE BROWNIE
300g (10½oz) dark chocolate,
  broken into small pieces
250g (9oz) butter
200g (7oz) caster sugar
4 medium eggs
150g (5¼oz) ground almonds
½ teaspoon salt

TO MAKE THE TOPPING
100g (3½oz) white chocolate
100g (3½oz) fresh raspberries,
  or 10g (½oz) freeze-dried

You will need a probe thermometer
  for the pâtes de fruits

GLUTEN FREE

Pictured on page 62.

Preheat the oven to 160°C fan/320°F/gas 4 and line your 22 x 33 x 5cm (8½ x 13 x 2in) baking tray (sheet pan), see page 7.

To make the pâtes de fruits, line a small loaf pan with siliconized baking parchment (the smaller the tray, the chunkier the cubes will be; a wide, shallow tray will give you ribbons rather than cubes). Put the raspberries in a blender and whizz them into a purée, then strain them through a sieve, pushing the pulp through with the back of a spoon.

Put the raspberry purée in a heavy-based saucepan over a medium–high heat. Mix 10g (½oz) of the caster (superfine) sugar with the pectin in a small jug and slowly add to the pan, whisking all the while. Next add the glucose, followed by the remaining sugar, continuing to whisk. Using a probe thermometer, heat the mixture to 107°C (225°F).

Meanwhile, rest a spoon on a flat surface and add the citric acid to the bowl of the spoon, then dissolve it by adding a few drops of water. Once the raspberry mixture is up to temperature, add the citric acid mixture, briefly whisk together, then instantly pour this into the lined loaf pan. Leave to cool completely (this will take about half an hour), then slice into small cubes.

Melt the chocolate and butter in a bain-marie (see page 8). Once melted, pour into a large mixing bowl or stand mixer and add the sugar, then beat in the eggs until the mixture becomes smooth, glossy and emulsified. Add the ground almonds and salt, and give it another quick mix, then add the cubes of pâtes de fruits and mix until combined.

Transfer the mixture to the lined tray and bake for 30 minutes, until the brownie is just set, but still has a little wobble in the middle. Leave to cool in the tray.

Once the brownie has cooled, you can make the tempered white chocolate topping. Gently melt two thirds of the white chocolate in a bain-marie until it just becomes runny, then take the bowl off the heat and add the remaining chocolate. Keep mixing until all the chocolate has melted. Remove the brownie from the tray and place on a chopping board. Working quickly, use a fork to drizzle thin lines of chocolate over the brownie, and before the chocolate sets, sprinkle with fresh or freeze-dried raspberries to add that eye-popping colour and salivating acidity. If the white chocolate becomes too stiff to drizzle, then put it back on a gentle heat to loosen up.

Best eaten at room temperature. This will keep for a week in an airtight container in the fridge.

CREAM TEA BROWNIE

When it comes to cream teas, people usually expect us to care about the whole Devon versus Cornwall 'cream or jam first' debate, as we're from Devon. Frankly, we couldn't give a toss, and have made up our own rules while the two counties battle it out. This is a cobbler brownie, where the scone mix is baked on top. You'll need to mix the cobbler after the brownie, as the acid (vinegar) starts to set off the raising agent straight away. Time is of the essence.

TO MAKE THE BROWNIE
300g (10½oz) dark chocolate, broken into pieces
300g (10½oz) butter
250g (9oz) caster (superfine) sugar
5 medium eggs
200g (7oz) ground almonds
10g (½oz) cocoa powder
1 teaspoon salt
200g (7oz) strawberry jam

TO MAKE THE SCONE MIX
175g (4¼oz) self-raising flour
1 teaspoon baking powder
45g (1⅗oz) butter, cut into cubes
2 tablespoons caster sugar
a pinch of salt
90ml (3fl oz) whole milk
5ml (1 teaspoon) white vinegar
1 egg, beaten, or 3 tablespoons whole milk, for an egg or milk wash (optional)

Pictured on page 63.

Preheat the oven to 160°C fan/320°F/gas 4 and line your 22 x 33 x 5cm (8½ x 13 x 2in) baking tray (sheet pan), see page 7.

Start by making your brownie. Melt the chocolate and butter together in a bain-marie (see page 8), stirring occasionally until they are combined and silky smooth. Pour into a large mixing bowl or stand mixer and add the sugar. Give it a quick stir, then beat in your eggs until the mixture becomes smooth, glossy and emulsified. Fold in the ground almonds, cocoa powder and salt until well combined, then pour the mixture into your lined tray.

Dollop the jam on top in spoonfuls, in a random fashion, then set aside while you make the scone mix.

Combine the flour and baking powder in a mixing bowl and add the cubes of butter. Rub the flour and butter with your fingers to make a crumble mixture, then add the sugar and salt. Mix the milk and vinegar together in a jug, then pour this into the scone mixture. Combine with a fork to form a wet dough. Dollop the dough over the brownie mixture, between the blobs of strawberry jam.

If you want that golden look, brush some milk or egg wash over the scone blobs, then bake for 30–40 minutes. You'll know it's ready when the scones are nice and crusty and the brownie has a little wobble in the centre. Obviously serve with some clotted cream from Devon or Cornwall.

Best eaten still warm. This will keep for a week in an airtight container in the fridge.

Although not strictly traditional – and arguably verging on treason – serving this with some plump, ripe strawberries and with a dollop of crème fraîche will bring a freshness to this brownie. (Sorry, people of Devon and Cornwall; please send your death threats in the post.)

MARMALADE ON TOAST BROWNIE

If Paddington Bear ate brownies, he would surely choose these ones. This recipe is a great way to repurpose that ageing sourdough loaf, reduce wastage and add crunchy texture to a fudgy brownie. Making the brownie mix with a wholemeal (wholewheat), low-gluten wheat flour from a local miller will add some maltiness, but it's OK to just use plain (all-purpose) flour too.

2 big slices of sourdough (about 100g/3½oz), crusts removed, cut into large crouton-sized chunks
300g (10½oz) dark chocolate, broken into pieces
250g (9oz) butter
300g (10½oz) caster (superfine) sugar
5 medium eggs
200g (7oz) plain (all-purpose) flour
1 teaspoon salt
50g (1¾oz) candied orange peel (optional), or make your own (see page 156)
100g (3½oz) marmalade

NUT FREE

Pictured on page 62.

Preheat the oven to 100°C fan/210°F/gas ½ and line your 22 x 33 x 5cm (8½ x 13 x 2in) baking tray (sheet pan), as well as a baking sheet, see page 7.

Spread out the bread chunks on the baking sheet and bake for about 30 minutes until they're really crunchy and brittle, and have lost their chewiness (don't worry if there's a little colour on the bread; some toasty flavour is a good thing). Once done, remove from the oven and leave to cool, and increase the oven temperature to 150°C fan/300°F/gas 3½.

While the croutons are getting crunchy, melt the chocolate and butter in a bain-marie (see page 8) or in a heavy-based saucepan over a very low heat. Add the sugar and mix until it starts to dissolve.

Take off the heat and, once the chocolate has cooled down a little, add the eggs and beat until glossy. Next, sift in the flour and salt and lightly fold until combined, then stir in the candied orange peel (if using) and a handful of the croutons. Scrape down the sides of the mixing bowl and give it all a final mix.

Pour the brownie mixture into your lined tray and scatter the remaining sourdough croutons on top, pressing them down into the batter. Spoon teaspoon-sized dollops of marmalade on top and bake for 25–30 minutes. You want a bit of a wobble in the middle of the tray when it comes out of the oven, to get that fudgy texture.

Best eaten on the day it's baked as the toast can go chewy, but it will keep for 5 days in an airtight container in the fridge.

Serve warm with ice cream, or leave to cool, but this is best eaten while the bread is still crunchy.

CHOCOLATE ORANGE BROWNIE

We make a blood orange version of this in the bakery with *pâtes de fruits*, which requires a lot of work. If you want to test your skills, the recipe is in the Technical Section (see page 147). This simpler version allows you to make something similar without having to use a thermometer or hunt around for yellow pectin and citric acid. We tried making the jelly with lots of different thickening agents and found gelatine gave the best texture without tainting the orange flavour.

TO MAKE THE JELLY

300ml (10fl oz) cold orange juice
4 sheets of gelatine or 45g (1⅔oz) powdered gelatine
50g (1¾oz) caster (superfine) sugar

TO MAKE THE BROWNIE

285g (10oz) dark chocolate, broken into pieces
120ml (4fl oz) / (110g/3¾oz) rapeseed (canola) oil
220g (7¾oz) caster sugar
15g (½oz) cornflour (cornstarch)
25ml (¾fl oz) cold orange juice
175ml (6fl oz) hot orange juice
120g (4oz) ground almonds
80g (3oz) oat flour (gluten-free)
30g (1oz) cocoa powder
1 teaspoon salt

TO MAKE THE TOPPING

240g (8½oz) dark chocolate, broken into pieces

GLUTEN FREE

Pictured on page 62.

Preheat the oven to 160°C fan/320°F/gas 4 and line your 22 x 33 x 5cm (8½ x 13 x 2in) baking tray (sheet pan), see page 7.

To make the orange jelly, pour the cold orange juice into a heavy-based saucepan and add the gelatine sheets. Soak for a few minutes, then place over a medium heat and add the sugar. Stir with a spatula and bring to the boil for a couple of minutes, then take off the heat and set aside while you make the brownie.

Make the brownie base by melting the chocolate in a bain-marie (see page 8), then add the oil and leave to warm and merge evenly. Pour into a large mixing bowl or the bowl of your stand mixer, but leave the bain-marie on the heat with the water in the pan still simmering. Add the sugar to the chocolate and oil and combine.

In the same bowl you used for the bain-marie, mix together the cornflour (cornstarch) and cold orange juice. Once combined, add the hot orange juice, then place the bowl back on the simmering pan to thicken. Once the mixture has thickened, add it to the chocolate and sugar and mix on a high speed (or by hand) until glossy and fully emulsified. Now add the ground almonds, oat flour, cocoa powder and salt, and mix to combine.

Pour the batter into your lined tray and spread the brownie mix to the corners, making sure it's level. Bake for 30 minutes. When it's ready, it will look nice and firm on top with a small wobble in the middle.

Once the brownie is cooked, leave it to cool in the tray or pop it in the freezer for a few minutes to speed things up. Pour the runny orange jelly mixture over the top of the cooled brownie base, then pop it in the fridge to set. This will take up to 4 hours; it's good to leave it that long if you can, or even overnight.

When the jelly is firm, make the chocolate topping by gently melting two thirds of the dark chocolate in a bain-marie. As soon as it's melted, take the bowl off the heat and add the remaining chocolate to temper. Pour the tempered chocolate over the orange jelly before it cools. Leave to set before serving.

This is best eaten on the day it's made. Avoid letting this brownie hang around for too long, as the jelly tends to permeate moisture into the tempered chocolate.

MILLIONAIRE BROWNIE

Caramel shortbread or brownie? How about both? This is a fusion between two iconic cakes, to make a Frankenstein's monster of something hideously delicious. The ground cardamom adds a bit of complexity to the bake, but obviously it works without.

TO MAKE THE BASE

125g (4¼oz) butter, melted
250g (9oz) soft light brown sugar
1 medium egg
100g (3½oz) plain
   (all-purpose) flour
½ teaspoon ground cardamom
a pinch of salt

TO MAKE THE CARAMEL

100g (3½oz) sugar
100g (3½oz) golden syrup
150ml (5fl oz) double
   (heavy) cream
a pinch of salt
50g (1¾oz) chilled butter

TO MAKE THE BROWNIE

200g (7oz) dark chocolate,
   broken into small pieces
150g (5¼oz) butter
190g (6¾oz) caster sugar
3 medium eggs
125g (4¼oz) plain flour
1 tablespoon cocoa powder
1 teaspoon salt

NUT FREE

Preheat the oven to 180°C fan/350°F/gas 6 and line your 22 x 33 x 5cm (8½ x 13 x 2in) baking tray (sheet pan), see page 7.

Make the base by beating together the butter and sugar until pale and fluffy, then add the egg and mix together. Sift in the flour, ground cardamom and salt, and fold in until smooth. Spread into your lined tray using a spatula, making sure to get right into the corners. Bake for around 25 minutes, or until it is dark gold in colour. It might rise up around the edge in places, but that's OK. Set aside to cool, and reduce the oven temperature to 160°C fan/320°F/gas 4.

Next, make the caramel. Heat the sugar and golden syrup in a heavy-based saucepan over a medium heat until it has melted together and is bubbling. Whisk in the cream and a pinch of salt, along with 30g (1oz) of the butter, then increase the heat to high. Keep things bubbling until the caramel turns a deep golden colour. Test the caramel by putting a spoonful on a cold plate. Leave it for a minute, then check to see how firm it is. You want it to be firm, but still pliable. When the caramel is ready, whisk in the remaining 20g (¾oz) butter and remove from the heat. Pour the caramel over the cooked pastry base and spread it with a spatula, but not quite to the sides. Pop the tray in the fridge or freezer so the caramel can set while you mix the brownie.

Make the brownie by melting the chocolate and butter in a bain-marie (see page 8). Once melted, add to a large mixing bowl or the bowl of your stand mixer and start mixing, adding the sugar a bit at a time. Keep mixing until the sugar dissolves. Add the eggs and beat on a high speed (or by hand) until the mixture emulsifies and becomes glossy and smooth. Reduce your speed and add the flour, cocoa powder and salt. Scrape down the sides of the bowl with a spatula, then give it another light mix to make sure everything is fully combined.

Pour the brownie mixture over the set caramel and spread it out to ensure it's level. Bake for 20–25 minutes and leave to cool in the tray before transferring to a chopping board and slicing. Enjoy in small slices with a cup of tea.

Best eaten at room temperature. This will keep for a week in an airtight container in the fridge.

A teaspoon of miso added to the caramel can add another dimension. You could also try replacing the brownie here, with another brownie recipe, such as the Rye or Almond (see pages 74 and 52): you'll need about 800g (1lb 12oz) of brownie mix in total.

FRENCH CARAMEL BROWNIE

It took a lot of trial and error to get this right, mainly due to the brownie being held up with ground almonds, which meant that there was no gluten for the caramel to joyfully cling to, giving up all pretence of being a solid, chewy entity. We solved this by making a set caramel that can hold its own. This recipe doesn't use a thermometer, so you have to use a keen eye and a good nose for burning sugar: you're wanting to hit that deep orange colour where you just start to smell hints of toffee.

TO MAKE THE FRENCH CARAMEL

80g (3oz) golden syrup
110g (3¾oz) caster
  (superfine) sugar
100ml (3½fl oz) double
  (heavy) cream
a pinch of salt
40g (1½oz) chilled butter

TO MAKE THE BROWNIE

375g (13¼oz) dark chocolate,
  broken into small pieces
375g (13¼oz) butter
300g (10½oz) caster sugar
6 medium eggs
225g (8oz) ground almonds
½ teaspoon fine salt
½ teaspoon sea salt flakes

You will need two baking trays
  (sheet pans) for this recipe

GLUTEN FREE

We also feel it's our duty to remind you about caramel burns – these are the worst, so don't touch the stuff with your finger, however tempting it may be, and best to keep kids out of the kitchen.

Preheat the oven to 160°C fan/320°F/gas 4 and line two 22 x 33 x 5cm (8½ x 13 x 2in) baking trays (sheet pans), see page 7.

To make the French caramel, heat the golden syrup and sugar in a heavy-based saucepan over a medium heat, tilting the pan from side to side so the melting sugar and golden syrup get acquainted. Bubble away in the pan for a few minutes until the contents begin to darken and give off a whiff of toffee. At this point, whisk in the cream and salt, along with half of the butter. Keep it bubbling away until the colour of the caramel becomes as dark as you dare, then whisk in the remaining butter until it's fully melted. Pour the hot caramel into one of your prepared trays and pop it in the freezer to set – this way, you can use it much sooner.

Now make the brownie mix by melting the chocolate and butter together in a bain-marie (see page 8), stirring occasionally, until they are combined and silky smooth. Pour the melted chocolate and butter into a large mixing bowl or the bowl of your stand mixer and add the sugar. Give it a quick stir, then beat in the eggs until the mix emulsifies, becoming smooth and glossy and starting to pull away from the sides of the bowl without sticking to it. Finally, fold in the ground almonds and fine salt until fully combined, then pour the mixture into your second lined tray.

By this point, the caramel should be brittle enough to smash into shards, but if it's soft, you can cut it into slithers and chunks and place them on top of the brownie mix. A random pattern is good. If you do have shards, stick them upright into the batter, so they melt down into pools, but still reach deep into the brownie.

Bake for 35–40 minutes. The brownie should be just cooked when you take it out, with a little wobble in the middle, and the caramel will bubble up a bit at the sides. Allow it to fully cool in the tray, then sprinkle some sea salt flakes over the top and serve.

Best eaten once fully cooled. This will keep for 2 weeks in an airtight container in the fridge.

To make a more refined version of the caramel used in this recipe, pick up a thermometer and head over to page 149 in the Technical Section. If you're really struggling to make a set caramel, you can just bake the brownie without it and then pour your liquid caramel over the top when serving.

CREAM CHEESE BROWNIE

This is such a popular combination, it even has its own appreciation day in the US. On 10 February – National Cream Cheese Brownie Day – you can join other enthusiasts and revel in its decadent goodness. It's all about the contrast with this one: monochromatic flavours and textures. If you are tempted to add nuts, we suggest macadamias – with their creamy texture, they make a great choice.

TO MAKE THE CREAM CHEESE

300g (10½oz) cream cheese
  (use supermarket own-brand)
70g (2½oz) caster
  (superfine) sugar
1 medium egg
1 teaspoon vanilla extract

TO MAKE THE BROWNIE

300g (10½oz) dark chocolate,
  broken into pieces
225g (8oz) butter
285g (10oz) caster sugar
4 medium eggs
200g (7oz) plain (all-purpose) flour
1 tablespoon cocoa powder
1 teaspoon salt

NUT FREE

Preheat the oven to 160°C fan/320°F/gas 4 and line your 22 x 33 x 5cm (8½ x 13 x 2in) baking tray (sheet pan), see page 7.

To make the cream cheese for marbling, put the cream cheese in a large mixing bowl or the bowl of your stand mixer with the sugar and beat until smooth, then add the egg and vanilla. Continue mixing until fully combined, then set aside in a clean bowl.

Next, make the brownie by melting the chocolate and butter together in a bain-marie (see page 8). Pour the melted chocolate and butter into a large mixing bowl, or the bowl of your stand mixer, and add the sugar a bit at a time. Keep mixing until the sugar dissolves, then add the eggs and beat on a high speed (or by hand) until the mixture emulsifies and becomes glossy and smooth. Reduce your speed and add the flour, cocoa powder and salt. Scrape down the sides of the bowl with a spatula, then give it another light mix to get everything fully combined. Pour the mixture into your lined tray.

While the brownie mix is still warm, dollop spoonfuls of the cream cheese mixture on top and then create swirling patterns using a toothpick or the handle of a teaspoon. If you're not feeling confident in getting sexy swirls, then you can just drag the toothpick up the rows of the dollops, as if you're plotting a route through them, then back down the other row. This will give a nice flowing look to the top.

Bake for 30–40 minutes. If it's getting too dark, cover the cake with a sheet of foil towards the end of cooking. Leave to cool in the tray, then transfer to a chopping board before serving.

Best eaten at room temperature. This will keep for a few days in the fridge in an airtight container, but it's better to eat it within a couple of days.

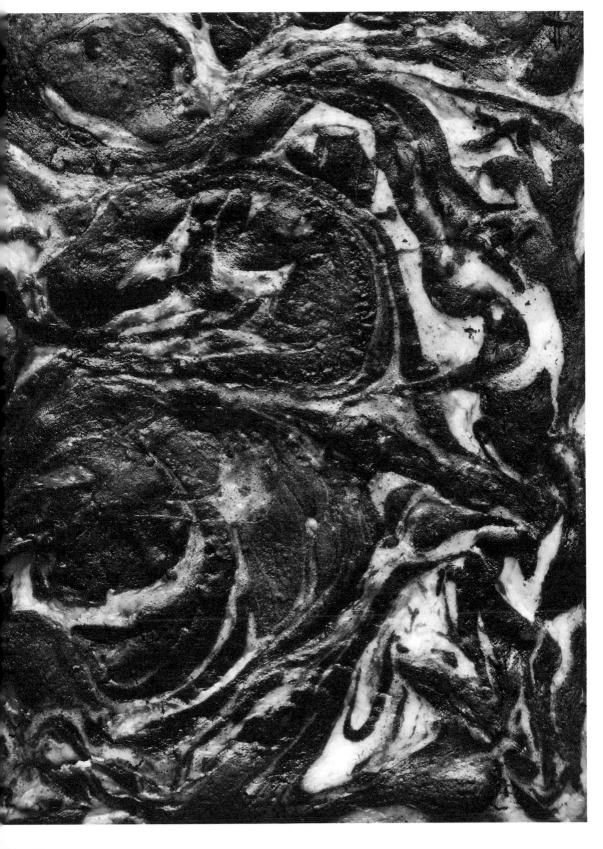

THE AMBASSADOR'S BROWNIE

If you're planning a party for the Ambassador and you suddenly realize there's a worldwide shortage of Ferrero Rocher, then fear not. This recipe will get you out of a bind. If you're less into hazelnuts than the Ambassador, you could use an almond praline and ground almonds instead – both are delicious. It's also totally cool to buy tubs of praline, but they are expensive, so we've included a recipe to make your own.

TO MAKE THE PRALINE PASTE
100g (3½oz) whole hazelnuts
90g (3¼oz) caster
(superfine) sugar
30ml (2 tablespoons) water
a pinch of salt
1 teaspoon rapeseed (canola) oil
(optional)

TO MAKE THE BASE
380g (13½oz) dark chocolate,
broken into pieces
150ml (5fl oz) / (135g/4¾oz)
rapeseed oil
285g (10oz) caster sugar
20g (¾oz) cornflour (cornstarch)
35ml (1¼fl oz) cold water
185ml (6¼fl oz) boiling water
150g (5¼oz) ground hazelnuts
100g (3½oz) oat flour (gluten-free)
40g (1½oz) cocoa powder
1 teaspoon salt

TO MAKE THE TOPPING
100g (3½oz) whole hazelnuts
250g (9oz) dark chocolate,
broken into pieces
100g (3½oz) praline (above)
edible gold leaf (optional)

VEGAN
GLUTEN FREE

Preheat the oven to 160°C fan/320°F/gas 4 and line your 22 x 33 x 5cm (8½ x 13 x 2in) baking tray (sheet pan), see page 7.

To make the praline paste, you can toast the hazelnuts beforehand and remove the husks by rubbing them in a dish towel (see page 43), but it's not essential. Start by adding the sugar and water to a heavy-based saucepan over a medium heat. Leave until the sugar dissolves, starts bubbling and then turns a deep orange colour, keeping a keen eye on it to avoid it going too dark. At this stage, add the hazelnuts and mix with a spatula, then tip everything out on to a sheet of baking parchment. Spread the mixture out and leave to cool completely; the paste will become a rock-solid caramel. Don't be tempted to touch this with your hands until cool.

Once cooled, break up the praline into smaller pieces. Pop the shards into a food processor, along with a pinch of salt, and blitz. Keep things whizzing until the nuts and caramel start to break down into a powder, then a paste. If this is taking too long, you can add a teaspoon of oil. Set aside.

To make the base, melt the chocolate in a bain-marie (see page 8), then add the oil and leave to warm and merge evenly. Pour into a large mixing bowl or the bowl of your stand mixer (leave the bain-marie on the heat with the water still simmering). Add the sugar to the chocolate and oil and combine.

In the same bowl you used for the bain-marie, mix together the cornflour (cornstarch) and cold water. Once they're combined, add the boiling water, then place the bowl back on the simmering pan to heat up as you stir. The mixture will thicken. Add this cornflour mixture to the chocolate and sugar and mix until glossy and fully emulsified. If the mixture splits, add a splash of boiling water to bring it together. Add the ground hazelnuts, oat flour, cocoa powder and salt, and mix to combine.

Pour the mixture into your tray and evenly spread it out to the corners. Bake for 30–40 minutes until just set, then leave to cool in the tray.

Once cool, make the topping by blitzing the hazelnuts in a food processor: you're aiming for little chunks, but not too fine. As before, you can toast the nuts first and remove the skin if you wish, but this isn't essential. Now melt the chocolate in a bain-marie and, once it's melted, add the nut pieces and praline paste. Remove from the heat and mix, then pour on to the brownie, spreading the mixture evenly. Let the praline chocolate mix set before cutting. Decorate with some edible gold leaf, if you fancy.

This will keep for 2 weeks in an airtight container in the fridge.

RYE BROWNIE

A high-quality chocolate with a decent level of acidity and bitterness adds deep layers of complexity to give this brownie an almost savoury edge. Cacao nibs bring a crunch to the party, but you can always use nuts instead. To really delve in at the deep end of the flavour pool, try some smoked sea salt sprinkled on top.

550g (1lb 3½oz) dark chocolate
200g (7oz) butter
6 medium eggs
350g (12oz) soft light brown sugar
200g (7oz) rye flour
1 teaspoon baking powder
½ teaspoon salt
40g (1½oz) raw cacao nibs
1 teaspoon sea salt flakes or
    smoked sea salt flakes

NUT FREE

Preheat the oven to 160°C fan/320°F/gas 4 and line your 22 x 33 x 5cm (8½ x 13 x 2in) baking tray (sheet pan), see page 7.

Melt the chocolate and butter in a bain-marie (see page 8), stirring occasionally until they are combined and silky smooth. Once melted, leave to cool a little.

In a stand mixer or large mixing bowl, beat the eggs on a high speed for about 5 minutes (or a bit longer if mixing by hand), adding the sugar a little at a time. The mixture should become frothy. Slowly pour in the melted chocolate and butter mixture and mix until emulsified. Then add the rye flour, baking powder and salt and mix until combined.

Pour into your lined baking tray and sprinkle with the cacao nibs. Bake for 30 minutes until the brownie puffs up, but is still wobbly. Allow to cool in the tray, then sprinkle with the sea salt flakes.

This will keep for 2 weeks in an airtight container in the fridge.

With all the seriousness of this brownie, it's sometimes fun to take it down a notch with a drizzle of Soft Caramel (see page 149).

SPELT BROWNIE

Not only is this brownie delicious, it also demonstrates how alternative ingredients can liberate you from the same old staples. After all the gluttony of this chapter, this is an attempt at a diversion from the pure filth that is cake. Whether this is actually healthier or not is debatable; it certainly feels a little more wholesome, though. The addition of beetroot (beet) adds to that sense of goodness, and the moisture and fibre bring something else to the party, making these a welcome change from the procession of standard brownies.

375g (13¼oz) dark chocolate, broken into pieces
250g (9oz) coconut oil
6 medium eggs
375g (13¼oz) coconut sugar
250g (9oz) wholemeal (wholewheat) spelt flour
1 teaspoon baking powder
1 teaspoon salt
120g (4oz) finely grated beetroot (beet) flesh
150g (5¼oz) walnuts (see notes)

Preheat the oven to 160°C fan/320°F/gas 4 and line your 22 x 33 x 5cm (8½ x 13 x 2in) baking tray (sheet pan), see page 7.

Melt the chocolate and coconut oil in a bain-marie (see page 8), stirring occasionally until they are combined and silky smooth. Once melted, leave to cool a little.

Meanwhile, in a large mixing bowl or stand mixer, beat the eggs on a high speed for about 5 minutes (or a bit longer if mixing by hand), adding the coconut sugar a little at a time. The mixture should become light and frothy. Slowly pour in the melted chocolate and oil mixture and mix until emulsified, then add the flour, baking powder and salt and slowly mix until combined. Stir in the beetroot (beet) and walnuts, then pour into the lined tray and bake for 30–35 minutes until the brownie puffs up, but is still wobbly. Leave to cool in the tray before slicing on a chopping board.

This will keep for 2 weeks in an airtight container in the fridge.

Spelt flour can sometimes be hard to find, so using normal wholemeal wheat flour works as a straight swap. Changing the coconut sugar to a blend of soft light brown and caster (superfine) sugar will also work if you can't find coconut sugar.

We like to leave the walnuts whole so they're more obvious in the bake. Lightly toasting them beforehand can give them a little more crunch and intensifies the nutty flavour.

AZTEC BROWNIE

This is a nod to chocolate's Aztec roots. It was originally consumed as a drink with spices, so we've tried to replicate some of those flavours here. The spice level is quite mellow – we've gone for a subtle back note, rather than a punch in the face – but feel free to add more should you prefer a bigger hit. Topping with edible gold could be seen as a little *nouveau riche*, but blinging up your brownie to tell the tale of Montezuma's treasure is still pretty fun.

350g (12oz) dark chocolate,
  broken into small pieces
350g (12oz) butter
280g (9¾oz) caster
  (superfine) sugar
6 medium eggs
200g (7oz) ground almonds
10g (½oz) cocoa powder
1 teaspoon ground cardamom
1 teaspoon ground cinnamon
1 teaspoon ground nutmeg
a pinch of mild chilli powder
80g (3oz) crystallized ginger
1 teaspoon salt
edible gold paint or edible gold
  leaf (optional)

GLUTEN FREE

Preheat the oven to 160°C fan/320°F/gas 4 and line your 22 x 33 x 5cm (8½ x 13 x 2in) baking tray (sheet pan), see page 7.

Make the brownie mix by melting the chocolate and butter together in a bain-marie (see page 8), stirring occasionally until they are combined and silky smooth. Pour into a large mixing bowl or the bowl of your stand mixer and add the sugar. Give it a quick stir, then beat in your eggs until the mixture emulsifies, becoming smooth and glossy and starting to pull away from the sides of the bowl without sticking to it. Finally, fold in your ground almonds, cocoa powder, spices, crystallized ginger and salt. Mix until fully combined, then pour into your lined tray.

Bake for 30 minutes. The brownie should be just cooked when you take it out, with a little wobble in the middle. Leave to cool in the tray and decorate with some edible gold paint or gold leaf, if you fancy.

Best eaten once fully cooled. This will keep for 2 weeks in an airtight container in the fridge.

Other spices worth considering in the mix are ground star anise, cloves or ginger – just go easy on these, as they can dominate. A good whack of vanilla can bring a more floral, gentle note, too.

FLOURLESS

Whether you're coeliac, gluten intolerant or gluten fatigued, this section showcases some excellent alternatives to traditional flour. A lot of gluten-free baking uses flour substitutes that don't add anything to your bake other than a sense of loss. We very rarely prescribe off-the-shelf gluten-free flour to our customers; we prefer to get them hooked on something with a little more texture and flavour. The best of the lot are ground almonds, either on their own or blended with polenta (cornmeal), oatmeal or buckwheat. Blending these ingredients is part of the experiment of baking and can yield different results, depending on what you're looking for in your crumb. Polenta, for example, will add bite and rigour to the cake's composition. Oats are naturally gluten-free, although they are often milled in the same place as other grains, meaning they pick up their gluten content by way of cross contamination. For this reason, it's best to seek out gluten-free oats, if you can. Oats add a delicious flavour and texture to many bakes, and if you really want some structure and bite, jumbo oats are the alphas, bringing a chest-beating dominance to the table. When you replace traditional flour with ingredients this tasty, we doubt the cake munchers will be pondering the digestion of wheat proteins; more likely, they'll be too busy eyeing up another slice.

FRUITY FLAPJACK

A terrazzo-looking flapjack, this is made with smaller, more delicate rolled oats. These give the mix a tight bind, which makes it a more portable creature, ideal for transporting in lunch boxes – or even as a pocket snack, if you want to bake it for a little longer to become a real tough cookie. Obviously, there is a lot going on here, and it really is a pick-and-mix kind of recipe, so play some jazz and create something unique.

210g (7½oz) butter
140g (5oz) golden syrup
45g (1⅗oz) honey
420g (14¾oz) gluten-free
  rolled oats
190g (6¾oz) mixed peel
120g (4oz) soft brown sugar
95g (3⅓oz) sunflower seeds
80g (3oz) dried apricots or
  sultanas (golden raisins)
80g (3oz) dried dates
35g (1¼oz) sesame seeds
finely grated zest of 1 large orange
  (see note)
30g (1oz) linseeds
1 teaspoon sea salt

GLUTEN FREE

Pictured on page 79.

Preheat the oven to 170°C fan/340°F/gas 5 and line your 22 x 33 x 5cm (8½ x 13 x 2in) baking tray (sheet pan), see page 7.

Melt the butter, golden syrup and honey together, either using a bain-marie (see page 8) or a heavy-based saucepan, until well combined, which should take around 10 minutes. Don't heat it for too long; the longer it heats, the harder the flapjack will be once baked. Next, combine all the remaining ingredients in a large mixing bowl, then add the melted mixture and combine using a wooden spoon.

Tip the mixture into your lined tray and spread it out evenly and firmly using the back of a spoon or a spatula. It's a good idea to press the flapjack to get that nice, dense power-bar texture. The best way to do this is to place a sheet of baking parchment over the mixture, then place another baking tray on top and press down. Remove the paper and bake the flapjack for about 30 minutes. The longer you bake it, the more it hardens up, so it's worth asking yourself: do you like it soft or hard? Leave to cool in the tray.

This will keep for 2 weeks in an airtight container in the fridge.

Zested oranges won't last long without the peel to protect the juice inside. It's probably worth just squeezing the juice right out there and then, and having a refreshing sip of juice while things are baking.

MANGO, YOGHURT & COCONUT FLAPJACK

This is inspired by the Indian drink mango lassi. It might not cool you down in quite the same way, but it's the perfect flapjack for a late summer evening snack. Pair with a crisp glass of gin and tonic or a soda and lime to really bring out the cardamom.

TO MAKE THE MANGO COMPOTE

450g (1lb) mango flesh
(about 3 mangos)
100g (3½oz) soft light brown sugar
juice of 1 lime

TO MAKE THE FLAPJACK

260g (9¼oz) golden syrup
200g (7oz) coconut oil
200g (7oz) soft light brown sugar
200g (7oz) desiccated (dried
shredded) coconut
500g (1lb 2oz) gluten-free oats
(ideally a mixture of jumbo
and rolled)
1 teaspoon salt

TO MAKE THE TOPPING

400g (14oz) white chocolate,
broken into small pieces
½ teaspoon ground turmeric
¼ teaspoon ground cardamom
200g (7oz) thick plain yoghurt
(10 per cent fat)

GLUTEN FREE

Pictured on page 79.

Preheat the oven to 180°C fan/350°F/gas 6 and line your 22 x 33 x 5cm (8½ x 13 x 2in) baking tray (sheet pan), see page 7.

To make the mango compote, place the mango flesh, sugar and lime juice in a heavy-based saucepan over a medium heat. Cook for 10 minutes, or until the mango has broken down completely, then remove from the heat and set aside.

Next, make the flapjack. Melt the golden syrup, coconut oil and sugar together in a heavy-based saucepan over a low heat until the sugar has dissolved and everything has come together. Combine the remaining ingredients in a large bowl, then pour the melted mixture on top and mix thoroughly.

Weigh 900g (2lb) of the flapjack mixture into your lined tray and smooth down, ideally by covering with baking parchment and then pressing it with the base of another tin. You want a nice, even, level top for this layer, so use a lot of pressure as you press.

Next, spoon the mango compote over the base layer and spread level with a spatula. Top with the remaining flapjack mix, sprinkling it as evenly as possibly. Give this a light press all over with your hands so it relaxes a little into the mango.

Bake the flapjack for about 30 minutes, until it begins to turn golden.

To make the topping, melt the white chocolate in a bain-marie (see page 8), then remove from the heat. Stir in the spices, then add the yoghurt a spoonful at a time, stirring between each addition. Give it all a good final mix, then pour on top of the flapjack and leave to set. Leave to cool in the tray.

This will keep for 2 weeks in an airtight container in the fridge.

Try making the topping with a mix of vegan white chocolate and coconut yoghurt to make this flapjack vegan. Also, those cans of alphonso mango pulp are really good if you don't want to make the compote.

CHERRY & PISTACHIO CAKE

There's something really special about the pistachio and cherry combination in this cake. The relatively low sugar content allows them to shine, and the coconut stirred through the mixture adds another layer of texture. At the bakery, we make this cake with sour cherries, as they are readily available in bulk, but it turns out cherries of the sour variety are not that easy to buy in the shops. So, we've adapted a version for you with sweet cherries, which is arguably better. We also experimented with some other alternatives, which turned out great: see the notes below.

TO MAKE THE CAKE

150g (5¼oz) caster (superfine) sugar
150g (5¼oz) soft light brown sugar
6 medium eggs
300ml (10fl oz) / (270g/9½oz) sunflower oil or rapeseed (canola) oil
125g (4¼oz) fine polenta (cornmeal)
100g (3½oz) desiccated (dried shredded) coconut
325g (11½oz) ground almonds
1 teaspoon salt
500g (1lb 2oz) fresh cherries
50g (1¾oz) chopped pistachios, to top

GLUTEN FREE

Preheat the oven to 170°C fan/340°F/gas 5 and line your 22 x 33 x 5cm (8½ x 13 x 2in) baking tray (sheet pan), see page 7.

Start by adding both types of sugar and the eggs to a large mixing bowl or stand mixer with a paddle attachment. Slowly mix until fully combined, then increase your speed and gradually pour in the oil, mixing until the oil is fully emulsified with the eggs and sugar. Reduce your speed and add the polenta (cornmeal) and desiccated (dried shredded) coconut. Continue to mix until incorporated. Finally, add the ground almonds and salt, and mix until incorporated. Be sure to scrape down the sides and bottom of the bowl and give it a final mix in case any rogue sugar and oil are lurking at the deep end, then pour into your lined tray.

Now pit your cherries by digging your thumbs into them and pulling the flesh apart, discarding the stones; do this over a large bowl so you don't lose any juice. Things will probably get a little messy, but that's OK. Once you've finished, you should have about 450g (1lb) cherry flesh. Scatter the cherries evenly over the top of the cake batter, then pour over any juice left in the bowl.

Bake for 1 hour to start with; you may need to add more time if necessary. You are looking for a golden-brown colour to the cake, and for the cherries to be dry to the touch. The cherries will turn a very dark colour, but don't worry – they're not burnt. Remove the cake from the oven when you have reached the desired bake and immediately top with the chopped pistachios. Leave to cool in the tray or on a chopping board.

This will keep for a week in an airtight container in the fridge.

When cherries are out of season, or just unaffordable, there are some alternatives. Dried sour cherries will work: chop 150g (5¼oz) into small pieces, then add 250ml (8½fl oz) boiling water with 1 tablespoon cornflour (cornstarch) mixed in. Let the cherries soak up the water and thicken up while they cool. Tinned cherries in syrup will work, although they may taste a bit bland - 2 tins, drained, will give you about 400g (14oz). Just tear them up into pieces and scatter over the batter as above. Even a jar of cherry compote mixed with the juice of 1 lemon will make a nice-tasting cake: add a few blobs on top of the cake batter. Also, you could try this recipe with rhubarb, and swap the pistachios for toasted flaked almonds.

ZUCCHINI & LIME CAKE

Although we call them courgettes in the UK, zucchini sounds more exotic somehow – and besides, courgettes have an association with savoury food. Baking a cake with a vegetable that is light on flavour, a bit fibrous and water-laden might sound like it wouldn't work, but it actually brings a lot of subtlety to the party. When grated, the zucchini adds texture and binds the ingredients. Most importantly, though, it brings its own unique brand of wholesome moisture. If you're into it, an iota of cardamom is a really good addition to this cake to give it a little more complexity.

TO MAKE THE CAKE
6 medium eggs
375g (13¼oz) caster
  (superfine) sugar
300ml (10fl oz) / (270g/9½oz)
  rapeseed (canola) or sunflower oil
400g (14oz) ground almonds
250g (9oz) polenta (cornmeal)
20g (¾oz) poppy seeds
a pinch of salt
finely grated zest and juice of
  3 limes
350g (12oz) courgettes (zucchinis),
  topped, tailed and grated
  (you should get 300g/10½oz
  grated flesh)

TO MAKE THE TOPPING
200g (7oz) icing (confectioners')
  sugar
finely grated zest and juice of 1 lime

GLUTEN FREE

Preheat the oven to 170°C fan/340°F/gas 5 and line your 22 x 33 x 5cm (8½ x 13 x 2in) baking tray (sheet pan), see page 7.

To make the cake, mix together the eggs and sugar until they emulsify, then slowly add the oil, mixing between each addition. Now add the almonds, polenta (cornmeal), poppy seeds and salt and mix to combine.

Stir in the lime zest and juice, followed by the grated courgettes (zucchinis). Once combined, pour the mixture into your lined tray and bake for 50–60 minutes until golden on top. Remove from the oven and leave to cool in the tray before icing. If you're short on time (or just impatient), you can pop the cake in the freezer so it cools faster.

While the cake is cooling, sift the icing (confectioners') sugar into a bowl and add the lime juice. Mix well to make a runny, white icing. Leaving it to sit for a while will help it thicken up. When the cake is cool enough, remove from the tray and place on a chopping board, then pour the icing over the top and, before the icing has time to harden, sprinkle over the lime zest to add a splash of colour. Alternatively, a scattering of poppy seeds looks good, too.

Best eaten at room temperature. This will keep for a week when stored in an airtight container in the fridge.

Before cutting and squeezing, rolling the lime on a hard surface with the palm of your hand will help it to release more juice. This method applies to most citrus fruits.

GOOSEBERRY & ELDERFLOWER CAKE

There's a fleeting beauty to the ingredients in this cake, and the chances of making it entirely with freshly foraged swag are slim, but there is a small window of opportunity in June (in the UK), where you can pick the gooseberries and elderflower together. If that's not a possibility, then frozen gooseberries are your friends, and some toasted almonds make a great alternative to the elderflowers. Shop-bought cordial is totally fine, although a little too syrupy. To make your own, see page 157 in the Technical Section.

TO MAKE THE CAKE
500g (1lb 2oz) gooseberries, roughly quartered (if you're using frozen berries, allow them to soften slightly before cutting)
150g (5¼oz) polenta (cornmeal)
250g (9oz) soft butter
125g (4¼oz) caster (superfine) sugar
125g (4¼oz) soft light brown sugar
5 medium eggs
200g (7oz) ground almonds
150ml (5fl oz) plain yoghurt
2 teaspoons elderflower cordial
juice of ½ lemon
2½ teaspoons baking powder

TO MAKE THE SYRUP
juice of 1½ lemons
50g (1¾oz) caster sugar
1 tablespoon elderflower cordial

TO MAKE THE ICING
50g (1¾oz) gooseberries
300g (10½oz) icing (confectioners') sugar
1 tablespoon elderflowers, or 40g (1½oz) toasted almonds

GLUTEN FREE

Pictured on page 85.

Preheat the oven to 160°C fan/320°F/gas 4 and line your 22 x 33 x 5cm (8½ x 13 x 2in) baking tray (sheet pan), see page 7.

To make the cake, toss the chopped gooseberries and polenta (cornmeal) together in a bowl, then set aside to let them get acquainted. In a large mixing bowl or stand mixer, cream together the butter and both sugars until fluffy, then add the eggs and beat until emulsified. Add the almonds, yoghurt, elderflower cordial, lemon juice and baking powder, along with the gooseberry and polenta mixture. Mix until fully combined, then pour into your lined tray. Use a spatula to level the mixture and bake for 45 minutes or until a knife inserted into the centre comes out clean.

While that's baking, make the syrup. In a heavy-based saucepan over a low heat, gently heat the lemon juice and sugar for a few minutes until the sugar has dissolved. Remove from the heat and add the elderflower cordial, then set aside. When the cake comes out of the oven, give the syrup a quick stir and pour it evenly over the top, then set aside to cool in the tray.

To make the icing, put the gooseberries and icing (confectioners') sugar in a food processor or blender and whizz until smooth. Once the cake is cool, lift on to a chopping board using the edges of the baking paper, then drizzle the icing all over the cake and sprinkle over the elderflowers or toasted almonds.

Best eaten at room temperature. This will keep for a week in an airtight container in the fridge.

With all the flavours of a New Zealand Sauvignon Blanc, this cake pairs perfectly with a glass of wine.

Best not to use dried elderflowers: they are OK for making tea, but will look a little sorry on a cake.

RICE PUDDING CAKE

Not exactly the food of the gods, but more a mash-up between a *torta di riso* and the tins of rice pudding manufactured right here in Devon under the brand name Ambrosia. This may be a hybrid, but it's still a very worthy and delicious cake-cum-pudding. There are some obvious adaptations to play with, like infusing the milk with citrus peel, or adding some dried fruit, but try this simple version first. This starts life as a rice pudding, and would be delicious served straight-up, but baking it as a cake adds a completely different dimension.

1.5 litres (50¾fl oz) whole milk
1 tablespoon vanilla paste
   or 1 pod, halved lengthways
2 bay leaves
a pinch of ground cinnamon
a grating of nutmeg
300g (10½oz) gluten-free pudding
   rice or risotto (arborio) rice
6 medium eggs
150g (5¼oz) caster
   (superfine) sugar
1 tablespoon honey or golden syrup
1 teaspoon salt
200ml (7fl oz) double
   (heavy) cream

GLUTEN FREE
NUT FREE

Preheat the oven to 180°C fan/350°F/gas 6 and line your 22 x 33 x 5cm (8½ x 13 x 2in) baking tray (sheet pan), see page 7.

Combine the milk, vanilla paste or pod, bay leaves, cinnamon and nutmeg in a large, heavy-based saucepan over a low heat. Cook for about 10 minutes, stirring now and then so it doesn't burn. Add the rice and simmer on a low–medium heat for another 30 minutes, or until the rice soaks up some of the liquid and the mixture looks a bit like a wet risotto. You want the rice to retain some bite, so make sure you don't overcook it. Remove from the heat and leave to cool slightly.

While that cools, beat the eggs and sugar in a mixing bowl with a whisk until frothy, then add the honey and salt and stir to combine. Remove the bay leaves and vanilla pod (if using) from the cooled rice and stir in the cream, then add the rice mixture to the eggs and sugar. Gently fold together, taking care not to break up the rice too much. Pour the mixture into the prepared tray and bake for 1 hour. A skin will form on the top and the cake should be an even deep brown all over. Leave to cool in the tray.

This can be eaten cool from the fridge, reheated or fresh from the tray. It will keep for 5 days in an airtight container in the fridge.

This is delicious served warm with prunes or some tart jam and toasted pine nuts, but it's equally tasty served cold. Try frying a cold slice in butter until it goes golden on one side, then serve with a bit of vanilla ice cream. Also, if you're all out of cream, just melt in 100g (3½oz) butter and an extra 100ml (3½fl oz) milk.

LEMON POLENTA CAKE

OK, OK, we've been caught *in flagrante*, in bed with *The River Café Cookbook*. Joking aside, that book was a real inspiration to us, and over the last ten years we've adapted things enough to be able to call this our own. Of course, the finest Sicilian or Amalfi lemons will make this cake spectacular, but even when life gives you shitty lemons, you can still make a cake. Unwaxed lemons are best, but if you're in a bind, give waxed lemons a good scrub with some warm water to remove any nasties.

TO MAKE THE CAKE

400g (14oz) soft butter
400g (14oz) caster
  (superfine) sugar
6 medium eggs
400g (14oz) ground almonds
200g (7oz) polenta (cornmeal)
  (see note)
2 teaspoons vanilla extract
1 teaspoon salt
finely grated zest and juice of
  2 lemons

TO MAKE THE SYRUP

finely grated zest and juice of
  2 lemons
75g (2½oz) golden syrup
100g (3½oz) caster sugar

TO TOP

50g (1¾oz) shelled pistachios

GLUTEN FREE

Preheat the oven to 160°C fan/320°F/gas 4 and line your 22 x 33 x 5cm (8½ x 13 x 2in) baking tray (sheet pan), see page 7.

To make the cake, start by creaming the butter and sugar together in a large mixing bowl or stand mixer, then beat in the eggs. Add the ground almonds, polenta (cornmeal), vanilla and salt and mix at a brisk speed until it's all combined. Now add the lemon zest and juice and mix a little further to bring everything together. This cake needs to be well combined, so give the bowl a good scraping with a spatula and then a final stir to catch any mixture that's still clinging to the sides and threatening to upset the bake.

Pour into your lined tray and bake for about 50 minutes until it starts browning on top.

While that's in the oven, make the syrup. Place all the ingredients in a heavy-based saucepan over a medium heat and bring to the boil, continuing to stir until the sugar has dissolved. Remove from the heat as soon as it's all dissolved – you don't want to boil it for too long, as the syrup will become too thick and not soak into the cake. Strain the syrup through a sieve into a jug or bowl and set aside.

Prepare the pistachio nuts for topping the cake by blitzing lightly in a food processor. If you don't have one, you can fold the nuts in a dish towel and give them a light smashing with a rolling pin. You don't want them turning to green dust, so go easy.

While the cake is still hot from the oven and still in the tray, pour the syrup over the top and spread out evenly with a spatula, then sprinkle over the broken-up pistachios. Serve warm with a dollop of mascarpone cheese or crème fraîche.

This will keep for 2 weeks in an airtight container in the fridge.

We like to use a mix of quick-cooking polenta (cornmeal) and the normal, more coarse stuff. The blend will give the cake a better structure. A teaspoon of a raising agent can also fluff things up if you like a lighter cake.

ORANGE, OLIVE OIL & PECAN CAKE

The complex flavour of the olive oil really plays off the sweetness of the orange in this polenta (cornmeal) cake. A cold-pressed rapeseed (canola) oil would also work, bringing a hay-like flavour and grown-up bitterness. Adding some saffron will lend a noteworthy colour and earthy taste, but it isn't an essential part of the recipe, just a little bonus for the taste buds. Pecans are the perfect nut to pair with these flavours, bringing a distinctive, creamy yet crunchy texture with an undertone of bittersweetness. A splash of orange blossom water can add a floral note to this cake if you happen to have any kicking around, or you could add some orange extract if you want to enhance the orange over the olive oil.

TO MAKE THE SYRUP
finely grated zest and juice of
  1 orange
75g (2½oz) golden syrup
50g (1¾oz) caster
  (superfine) sugar
a tiny pinch of saffron (optional)

TO MAKE THE CAKE
390ml (13fl oz) / (350g/12oz)
  extra virgin olive oil
400g (14oz) caster sugar
6 medium eggs
400g (14oz) ground almonds
200g (7oz) polenta (cornmeal)
1 teaspoon salt
finely grated zest and juice of
  2 oranges

TO TOP THE CAKE
100g (3½oz) pecan nuts
1 teaspoon fennel seeds, toasted
  and crushed (optional)

GLUTEN FREE

Preheat the oven to 160°C fan/320°F/gas 4 and line your 22 x 33 x 5cm (8½ x 13 x 2in) baking tray (sheet pan), see page 7.

To make the syrup, combine all the ingredients in a heavy-based saucepan over a medium heat. Bring to the boil, stirring occasionally to dissolve the sugars. Remove from the heat and strain through a sieve (see note below) into a jug, then set aside.

To make the cake, combine the oil and sugar in a large mixing bowl or stand mixer on a medium speed. Add the eggs and continue to mix. Scrape down the sides of the bowl, then beat in the ground almonds, polenta (cornmeal), salt and the orange juice and zest, until everything is combined and you have a pleasingly fluffy batter.

Now prepare the pecans for the topping. Pulse them in a food processor or blender to break them up. If you don't have either of these, you can wrap them in a dish towel and smash with a rolling pin. Ideally you don't want pecan dust, so go gently.

Pour the cake mixture into your lined tray and spread out with a spatula to level the top. Scatter your pecans evenly across the top: there's no need to press them into the batter, as the cake will absorb them until they just peek through the crust. Bake for about 45–50 minutes until the cake is slightly domed at the edges and nicely browned.

Remove the cake from the oven and, while it's still hot and still in the tray, trickle the syrup over the top, spreading it out evenly using a pastry brush to cover all the pecans. Scatter over the fennel seeds (if using) to add a little something extra in terms of both flavour and aroma. Leave to cool in the tray, then transfer to a chopping board for slicing.

This will keep for 2 weeks in an airtight container in the fridge.

When you've made the syrup, discard any pips from your sieve and then spread out the boiled bits of zest on a baking tray. Bake on a low heat to make a quick candied peel.

GRAPEFRUIT & HONEY POLENTA CAKE

With this cake, the bitter and tart qualities of the grapefruit smack you in the chops, only to be instantly balanced by the sugar. Grapefruit in a cake is an unusual proposition, but that bitterness mellows into a background hum, with the flavour running through the whole cake while the honey offers a soothing note of sweetness. It's another variation of our polenta (cornmeal) cake, so you should be getting the idea of the slight alterations in technique and ingredients – why not try some of your own?

TO MAKE THE SYRUP

50g (1¾oz) syrup from the stem (preserved) ginger jar (see below)
50g (1¾oz) honey
finely grated zest and juice of 1 ruby grapefruit

TO MAKE THE CAKE

400g (14oz) soft butter
400g (14oz) caster (superfine) sugar
6 medium eggs
400g (14oz) ground almonds
200g (7oz) polenta (cornmeal)
1 teaspoon salt
finely grated zest and juice of 1 ruby grapefruit
190g (6¾oz) stem ginger from a jar

TO MAKE THE TOPPING

125g (4¼oz) thick full-fat plain yoghurt
125g (4¼oz) mascarpone
125g (4¼oz) icing (confectioners') sugar
1 ruby grapefruit, peeled and segmented (see note)
a drizzle of runny honey or stem ginger syrup (optional)

GLUTEN FREE

Preheat the oven to 160°C fan/320°F/gas 4 and line your 22 x 33 x 5cm (8½ x 13 x 2in) baking tray (sheet pan), see page 7.

Start by making the syrup. Place all the ingredients in a heavy-based saucepan over a medium heat. Bring to the boil, then strain through a sieve into a jug and set aside.

To make the cake, cream the butter and sugar in a large mixing bowl or stand mixer until light and fluffy, then add the eggs and combine. Next, beat in the ground almonds, polenta (cornmeal) and salt until everything comes together to form a light, smooth batter.

In a blender, blend the grapefruit zest and juice with the stem (preserved) ginger, then add this to the batter and mix a little further until combined. Pour into your lined tray and bake for about 45–50 minutes until it begins to brown on the top.

Remove the cake from the oven, and while it's still hot, pour the syrup over the top and gently spread with a spatula, trying not to damage the top of the cake. Now set the cake aside to cool in the tray while you make the topping.

In a large bowl, lightly beat together the yoghurt and mascarpone, then sift in the icing (confectioners') sugar and gently mix until well combined and lump-free. A whisk is good for this; an electric one is even better, if you have it.

Once the cake is cool, remove it from the tray and spread the icing evenly over the cake: we suggest you do this with the back of a spoon and create some peaks and troughs for a bit of drama. Lay the grapefruit segments over the cake in a random fashion, then, finally, add a light drizzle of runny honey or ginger syrup over the top.

This will keep for a week in an airtight container in the fridge.

To prep the grapefruit, top and tail it, then place one of the flat sides on a chopping board and cut down the sides, slicing off the peel (which you can save to make the Quasi Candied Citrus on page 156). Now slice the segments alongside the membrane for surgically precise segmented pieces.

BLOOD ORANGE POLENTA CAKE

OK, let's turn things upside down, flip everything on its head. Here's a cake that uses a now-familiar base recipe, but from a totally different perspective. Rather than finishing the cake with the syrup on top, this cake is baked on the syrup and turned out of the tray upside down. It's a fun way to get the moisture into the cake – and, thanks to the spectacular look of the blood oranges, it is also a thing of beauty. If you can't get hold of blood oranges, there is no reason why you couldn't try this with a mix of ruby red grapefruit, limes and lemons.

TO MAKE THE CANDIED ORANGES

3 blood oranges
100ml (3½fl oz) cold water
200g (7oz) caster (superfine) sugar
½ teaspoon ground cardamom

TO MAKE THE CAKE

400g (14oz) soft butter
400g (14oz) caster sugar
6 medium eggs
400g (14oz) ground almonds
200g (7oz) polenta (cornmeal)
finely grated zest and juice of
   1 blood orange
1 teaspoon salt

GLUTEN FREE

Preheat the oven to 180°C fan/350°F/gas 6 and line your 22 x 33 x 5cm (8½ x 13 x 2in) baking tray (sheet pan), see page 7.

Begin by preparing the candied oranges. Top and tail two of the oranges and slice as thinly as you can into rounds, so they look like bicycle wheels. Cut about two thirds of the slices in half again across the middle to create half-moons, then arrange the slices in your lined baking tray – there will be some overlapping, but it doesn't matter. Next, squeeze the juice of the third orange into a heavy-based saucepan over a high heat. Add the water, sugar and ground cardamom, then bring to the boil for a few minutes. Remove from the heat and pour the syrup over the orange slices in the tray. Pop in the oven for 30 minutes.

Once they're cooked, remove from the oven and reduce the oven temperature to 160°C fan/320°F/gas 4. Pop the tray in the freezer to chill things down. Once they're cool enough to touch, arrange the slices by standing the half-moons upright around the edges of the tray, with the flat edges on the bottom. Ideally, you would then be able to pair each of these with another half-moon on the base of the tray, so each one sits at a right angle to another half. Then arrange the remaining slices across the base of the tray so there are no gaps: it's OK if some of the slices overlap.

To make the cake, cream the butter and sugar in a large mixing bowl or stand mixer. Add the eggs and mix, then beat in the ground almonds until the mixture is well combined and fluffy. Add the remaining ingredients and mix gently to combine. Scrape down the sides of the bowl and give everything a final mix, then very carefully pour the batter over the arranged orange slices, using the cake mix to hold up the slices around the edges. Make the surface as level as you can, then bake for 45–50 minutes until the top begins to turn brown.

When the cake is ready, allow it to cool in the tray or pop it in the freezer if you're feeling impatient. Place something flat, like a chopping board, on top of the cake and press the two together, then flip them over with one hand underneath the baking tray and the other on top of the board. Lift the baking tray off gently and carefully peel away the baking parchment. Cut the cake with a razor-sharp knife: it helps to chill the cake first if you're struggling to cut through the orange slices without damaging the cake.

This will keep for a week in an airtight container in the fridge.

THE NUTCRACKER CAKE

Someone once said they hate Christmas food, and if it was really that good, we'd eat it all year round. That might be true, and if all the marzipan, dried fruit, mixed (pumpkin pie) spice and brandy cream is getting too much next festive season, then this version of an Italian hazelnut torte (*torta di nocciole*) is a nice change of pace after all those suet-based puddings and heavy pastry. Although packed with nuts and rather dense, it somehow feels like a lighter option, and is delicious served with mascarpone cream. The cake begins its life in the form of a *zabaglione*, a kind of light and frothy Italian custard made with booze, but then the nut boulders are tipped in, and out of the rubble comes this architectural beauty with the nuts concreted in the structure, glistening like terrazzo tiles.

TO MAKE THE CAKE
6 medium eggs
125g (4¼oz) caster
  (superfine) sugar
125g (4¼oz) soft light brown sugar
1 teaspoon vanilla extract
50ml (1¾fl oz) Somerset cider
  brandy or Frangelico – or just raid
  the drinks cabinet (optional)
300g (10½oz) dark chocolate,
  broken into small pieces
100g (3½oz) butter
250g (9oz) whole hazelnuts
250g (9oz) walnut pieces
100g (3½oz) ground almonds
2 teaspoons ground cinnamon
50g (1¾oz) candied orange peel,
  finely chopped (see page 156
  to make your own)
½ teaspoon salt

TO TOP
15g (⅔oz) icing (confectioners')
  sugar (or more if you like)

GLUTEN FREE

Preheat the oven to 150°C fan/300°F/gas 3½ and line your 22 x 33 x 5cm (8½ x 13 x 2in) baking tray (sheet pan), see page 7.

To make the cake, crack the eggs into a large mixing bowl or stand mixer and beat until foaming like a bubble bath. Add both types of sugars, a little at a time, beating between each addition, followed by the vanilla and the booze (if you fancy it).

Melt the chocolate and butter together in a bain-marie (see page 8). Once melted, slowly add to the egg mixture with the mixer still running. Things should emulsify into a sea of glossy goodness.

Put the hazelnuts and walnut pieces in a food processor (don't worry about the skin; a touch of bitterness brings balance). Whizz the machine on and off until the mixture has a gravelly texture (it doesn't matter if some of the hazelnuts are still whole). If you don't have a food processor, try wrapping the nuts in a dish towel and smashing with a rolling pin.

Place the broken nuts in a separate mixing bowl, along with the ground almonds, cinnamon, candied orange peel and salt. Mix to combine.

Transfer the beaten egg and chocolate mixture to the bowl of nuts and stir through so everything is coated and even. Pour this mixture into your lined tray and bake for 30 minutes until a knife inserted into the centre comes out clean. If the cake is browning too quickly, reduce the oven temperature slightly or cover with foil.

Leave to cool in the baking tray, then remove the cake from the tray and dust generously with icing (confectioners') sugar. If you really want to, you could add some hideous decorations or a few holly leaves to bring some festive cheer.

Best served at room temperature or warm (see below). This will keep for two weeks when stored in an airtight container in the fridge.

Serving this warm will soften the texture slightly and make it feel more like a dessert, especially if you add a dollop of mascarpone on the top to give a nod to its Italian heritage.

BURNT BASQUE CHEESECAKE

This sunken burnt cake may look like your first attempt at baking in a home economics class – but that's exactly how it should look. The style comes from the Basque region in Spain, and is fast becoming world-renowned on dessert menus. Obviously it's best to visit the country yourself to scoff the real deal, but failing that, break out the Pedro Ximenez and have a bash yourself.

800g (1lb 12oz) cream cheese
   (use supermarket own-brand),
   at room temperature
250g (9oz) caster
   (superfine) sugar
6 medium eggs
25g (1oz) cornflour (cornstarch)
300g (10½oz) sour cream
a pinch of salt
1 teaspoon vanilla paste,
   or seeds from 1 vanilla pod

GLUTEN FREE
NUT FREE

Preheat the oven to 220°C fan/430°F/gas 9 and line your 22 x 33 x 5cm (8½ x 13 x 2in) baking tray (sheet pan), see page 7.

In a large mixing bowl or stand mixer, mix together the cream cheese and sugar for a few minutes, so the sugar starts to dissolve. Add the eggs one at a time, beating between each addition until fully combined. While mixing, gradually add the cornflour (cornstarch), followed by the sour cream, salt and vanilla.

Tip the mixture into your lined tray and give it a wiggle and a jiggle, then slam the tray firmly on the worktop a couple of times to knock out any big air pockets. Bake for 35–40 minutes until the top is a very dark brown. There should still be a wobble in the middle of the cake when it comes out of the oven. Just to forewarn you, the cake will sink in the middle, but it's all part of the plan.

Leave to cool in the tray. This cake can be eaten at room temperature after cooling down, but it tastes even better cold from the fridge. Either way, try serving with some stewed fruit: gooseberries or rhubarb both work well.

This will keep for 4 days in an airtight container in the fridge.

Adding a biscuit (cookie) or pastry base could cause rioting in Spain. Go on, we dare you!

GAZILLIONAIRE SLICE

This is our take on a caramel slice, which is an indulgence many of us find hard to resist.

We really wanted to make a cake that ticked all the boxes and punched all the major allergens in the face. It took a few years to develop, but here it is: a vegan, gluten-free, nut-free caramel slice that's good enough to make anyone forget they even had dietary requirements. Especially if they're made up.

TO MAKE THE ANZAC COOKIE BASE

100ml (3½fl oz) / (90g/3¼oz) rapeseed (canola) oil
100g (3½oz) golden syrup
200g (7oz) soft light brown sugar
½ teaspoon bicarbonate of soda (baking soda)
2 tablespoons water
200g (7oz) gluten-free flour
120g (4oz) gluten-free rolled oats
80g (3oz) desiccated (dried shredded) coconut
1 teaspoon salt

TO MAKE THE DATE CARAMEL

150g (5¼oz) coconut oil
125ml (4¼fl oz) soy milk
450g (1lb) chopped dates in rice flour (available in most health-food stores)
75g (2½oz) golden syrup
½ teaspoon salt or miso

TO MAKE THE TOPPING

350g (12oz) dark chocolate, broken into small pieces
30g (1oz) coconut oil

VEGAN
GLUTEN FREE
NUT FREE

Preheat the oven to 160°C fan/320°F/gas 4 and line your 22 x 33 x 5cm (8½ x 13 x 2in) baking tray (sheet pan), see page 7.

First, prepare the Anzac cookie. Gently heat the rapeseed (canola) oil, golden syrup and soft light brown sugar together in a large heavy-based saucepan over a low heat. While this mixture is heating, combine the bicarbonate of soda (baking soda) and water in a cup and add to the pan, along with the dry ingredients. Mix it all together with a wooden spoon until fully combined. Transfer the Anzac mixture to your lined tray, spreading it out evenly across the base, and bake for 30 minutes until it turns a nice golden colour and puffs up slightly. Set aside to cool and firm up.

Next, make the date caramel. Melt the coconut oil in a heavy-based saucepan over a low heat, then add the soy milk and increase the heat. When it's close to boiling point, chuck in the chopped dates and reduce the heat back to low. Leave for 5 minutes, stirring occasionally, then remove from the heat and allow to cool a little before blending with a stick blender or in a food processor. Add the golden syrup and salt and blend a little further, until fully combined. You want the coconut oil to be fully absorbed with none leaching out. Pop in the fridge or freezer to cool a little. When it's cool enough to touch, spread the date caramel over the chilled Anzac base, making sure it's level.

Next, melt half the chocolate with the coconut oil in a bain-marie (see page 8), then remove from the heat and temper by adding the other half of the chocolate, stirring until you have a fully melted mixture. Pour this over the chilled date mixture and leave to set for 1 hour in the fridge before slicing.

Best eaten at room temperature. This will keep for 2 weeks in an airtight container in the fridge.

Get a super-crisp looking slice by using a hot knife to slice.

BOSS LEVEL

The recipes in this section require a little more skill for a slightly fancier pay-off. Fear not, though, we aren't talking hardcore patisserie: it's more like getting your yellow belt in judo. A few of the recipes will need some more in-depth prep and detailed planning, and you'll want to make sure you've got all the equipment ready to go and the ingredients weighed out, as the timings are key (although we're sure you do that anyway, as we suggested on page 15).

We love to see our cakes eaten at any point in the day, and this section particularly lends itself to dessert, with many of these featuring the addition of crème fraîche, custard, cream or ice cream. Enough of the pep talk – it's time you rolled up those sleeves, got that pinny on and made a mess.

MINCE PIE SLICE

This slice offers something a little lighter than a pastry-laden mince pie – and is so much tastier. It makes a good dessert, too, when served with a dollop of crème fraîche and a little clementine zested over the whole affair. Making mincemeat is a little bit of a faff, so buying a jar and adding some extra nuts and boozy bits is totally fine, and will turn the shop-bought stodge into something with a bit more flavour. Homemade is best if you have the time, though, so here is our recipe, which uses butter instead of suet. The shortbread biscuit base is a welcome change from pastry and makes for a solid foundation.

TO MAKE THE BASE

125g (4¼oz) butter
65g (2¼oz) caster
 (superfine) sugar
a pinch of salt
200g (7oz) plain (all-purpose) flour
 (wholemeal/wholewheat is
 good, too)

TO MAKE THE MINCEMEAT
[MAKES ABOUT 700G/1LB 9OZ]

50g (1¾oz) butter
75g (2½oz) soft light brown sugar
1 tart apple, grated (about
 100g/3½oz)
½ teaspoon ground cinnamon
½ teaspoon ground mixed
 (pumpkin pie) spice
180g (6¼oz) mix of sultanas, raisins,
 currants and dried cranberries
30g (1oz) mixed peel
20g (¾oz) almonds or hazelnuts,
 roughly chopped
finely grated zest and juice of
 1 lemon or orange
100ml (3½fl oz) booze (brandy,
 whisky or bourbon)
a pinch of salt

TO MAKE THE FRANGIPANE

200g (7oz) soft butter
200g (7oz) caster sugar
4 medium eggs
200g (7oz) ground almonds
50g (1¾oz) plain flour
a pinch of salt

TO TOP

icing (confectioners') sugar, to dust

Pictured on page 102.

Preheat the oven to 160°C fan/320°F/gas 4 and line your 22 x 33 x 5cm (8½ x 13 x 2in) baking tray (sheet pan), see page 7.

To make the base, melt the butter with the sugar in a large heavy-based saucepan over a low heat, then add the salt. Once the butter has melted, take the pan off the heat and add the flour, then combine to make a wet pastry. If it's not pliable, add a splash of water and mix a little more.

Press the mixture evenly into the lined tray, using a spatula or your hands. Try to get the pastry mix to come up the sides of the tray a little, as it will shrink a bit during the cooking process. Bake for 30 minutes until golden.

Meanwhile, make the mincemeat. Melt the butter and sugar in a large heavy-based saucepan over a low heat. Add the grated apple and spices and cook for 5 minutes, then add the dried fruit, mixed peel and nuts and stir. Add the lemon zest and juice, along with the booze and salt, and mix it all in. Remove from the heat and set aside.

For the frangipane, melt the butter in a heavy-based saucepan over a low heat, then transfer to a large mixing bowl or the bowl of your stand mixer. Add the sugar and mix together so it becomes fluffy, then add the eggs, one at a time, beating between each addition so it fully combines. Add the ground almonds, flour and salt, and mix well. Scrape down the sides of the bowl and give it all a final mix. It should be smooth and slightly runny.

When the base is out of the oven, top with the mincemeat, use a fork to rake and spread it out evenly to the edges, making sure it's level. Top this with the frangipane and level that out too, ideally with a pallet knife or spatula for a smooth finish. A fork is also useful for this: try to gently rake the frangipane to the edge without disturbing the mincemeat underneath, then smooth over the top. Increase the oven temperature to 170°C fan/340°F/gas 5 and bake for 30 minutes, or until the frangipane has risen slightly, turned golden and set.

Leave to cool in the tray, then dust with a snowstorm of icing (confectioners') sugar and cut into slices.

Serve this warmed up, just like a mince pie. It will keep for 2 weeks in an airtight container in the fridge. The mincemeat will keep for months in the fridge, so feel free to multiply the recipe, if you want to jar it up for another batch.

PANETTONE BREAD & BUTTER PUDDING CAKE

Do not make this with a perfectly good panettone: use an old one that's out of date or has been acquired after the Christmas hullabaloo at a heavy discount. Alternatively, you could make this with some white sliced bread, with the addition of some candied peel and dried fruit, and perhaps a splash of booze, a dollop of jam and some chunks of chocolate as an attempt to emulate the sweet Italian bread. Other enriched doughs, such as brioche or croissants, will also work a treat. The idea of this cake is to use up leftovers, and it's all about creating texture with something gooey encased in a layer of crunch.

TO MAKE THE CAKE

100g (3½oz) butter
100g (3½oz) caster (superfine) sugar
900g–1kg (2lb 4oz) panettone, sliced into 2cm (¾in) slices

TO MAKE THE CUSTARD

500ml (17fl oz) whole milk
1 teaspoon vanilla paste, or seeds from 1 vanilla pod
150g (5¼oz) butter
100g (3½oz) caster sugar
6 medium eggs

TO MAKE THE TOPPING

75g (2½oz) chopped hazelnuts
100g (3½oz) demerara sugar

Preheat the oven to 180°C fan/350°F/gas 6 and line your 22 x 33 x 5cm (8½ x 13 x 2in) baking tray (sheet pan), see page 7.

To make the cake, melt the butter in a heavy-based saucepan over a low heat, then mix in the caster (superfine) sugar. Create a base for the cake by taking some middle slices of the panettone, and placing them in the base of the lined tray. You want to use about 375g (13¼oz) of the panettone here. Squash the slices down with your hands, then pour the melted butter and sugar over the top so the panettone can soak up the butter. Pop it in the oven for 25 minutes to get a little brown and crispy as the sugar turns to caramel.

While the base is baking, make the custard. Warm the milk and vanilla in a heavy-based saucepan over a gentle heat. Just before the milk begins to simmer, take it off the heat and add the butter. In a large bowl, whisk together the caster sugar and eggs, then slowly add the hot milk and melted butter mixture, continuing to whisk. Tear up the rest of the panettone and add that to the bowl too. Mix it all together to create a silky, bready custard.

When the base is ready, pour this custard over the top, then sprinkle with some chopped hazelnuts and a sprinkling of demerara sugar and bake for 25 minutes.

The cake should have a slight wobble in the middle. It can be eaten warm like a pudding or left to cool and eaten like a cake. The double-baked base should give enough stability to lift the slice to your mouth to start the devouring process.

Best eaten on the day it's baked to retain the crunch, but it will keep for 4 days in an airtight container in the fridge.

Chocolate really works in this recipe too. A sneaky 100g (3½oz) of chocolate buttons or small broken shards hidden in the mix will create little pockets of chocolatey joy as they melt during the bake.

LUMBERJACK CAKE

The apple doesn't fall far from the tree, and this father figure of a recipe can spawn many similar creations. Eating this cake warm is like meeting a sticky toffee pudding all grown up, having developed character with the acidity from the apples. The butterscotch and coconut add texture and crunch, like a gravelly voice from smoking too many cigarettes.

TO MAKE THE CAKE

250g (9oz) dried chopped dates
1 teaspoon bicarbonate of soda
  (baking soda)
330ml (11¼fl oz) boiling water
500g (1lb 2oz) peeled, cored and
  cubed apples (about 4–5 apples)
175g (4¼oz) soft butter
300g (10½oz) caster
  (superfine) sugar
2 medium eggs
2 teaspoons vanilla extract
400g (14oz) plain
  (all-purpose) flour
1 teaspoon salt

TO MAKE THE TOPPING

75g (2½oz) butter
125g (4¼oz) soft light brown sugar
70g (2½oz) desiccated (dried
  shredded) coconut
100ml (3½fl oz) whole milk

NUT FREE

Preheat the oven to 170°C fan/340°F/gas 5 and line your 22 x 33 x 5cm (8½ x 13 x 2in) baking tray (sheet pan), see page 7.

To make the cake, place the chopped dates in a bowl, then add the bicarbonate of soda (baking soda). Pour in the boiling water. Add the cubed apples, then set aside to soak and cool for about 10 minutes.

Cream together the butter and sugar in a large mixing bowl or stand mixer, then add the eggs and vanilla extract and beat until fluffy and light. Now gently fold in the flour and salt, being careful not to over-mix. Next, add the apple and date mixture, including the soaking water, and combine, again being nice and gentle. Pour into your lined tray and bake for 40–50 minutes.

While the cake is baking, get started on the topping. Heat all the ingredients together in a heavy-based saucepan over a low heat until the butter melts and the coconut soaks up some of the milk. Give it a good stir until it thickens slightly, then set aside.

Check that the cake is ready: you'll know it's done when a knife inserted into the centre comes out clean-ish (it's a very pudding-like cake, so don't worry too much if there's a bit of mixture stuck on there). Pour the topping over the hot cake and spread it out evenly with a spatula, then return to the oven for a further 25 minutes until the top becomes golden brown. The more you caramelize it, the crunchier it'll be when it cools.

Best served warm with clotted cream, but still delicious cold with a cup of tea.

This will keep for 2 weeks in an airtight container in the fridge.

Cooking apples are good for this recipe, but tart eating apples work too. To cut wastage, pop the peelings in a jar and fill with a 5 per cent sugar syrup. Cover with a dish towel and leave for a couple of weeks to make vinegar.

LUMBERJILL CAKE

This cake was born out of a sticky situation: we were going to make a Lumberjack Cake (page 104), but we were all out of dates, so had to improvise with plums instead. Sometimes you need to make things up as you go along – like the name. It was originally called Plumberjack, but Lumberjill is a better marriage to her husband cake. More importantly, this is a good example of adapting a recipe, and will hopefully inspire you to make some changes of your own and mix things up. Just remember, it's not always as simple as a straight swap, as things like moisture content and texture need to be right, so a little bit of on-your-feet thinking is required.

TO MAKE THE CAKE

500g (1lb 2oz) peeled, cored and
    cubed apples (about 4-5 apples)
400g (14oz) fresh plums, stoned
    and quartered, skin left on
1 teaspoon bicarbonate of soda
    (baking soda)
175g (4¼oz) soft butter
300g (10½oz) caster
    (superfine) sugar
2 medium eggs
2 teaspoons vanilla extract
400g (14oz) plain
    (all-purpose) flour
1 teaspoon salt

TO MAKE THE TOPPING

75g (2½oz) butter
125g (4¼oz) soft light brown sugar
100ml (3½fl oz) whole milk
125g (4¼oz) flaked almonds

Preheat the oven to 160°C fan/320°F/gas 4 and line your 22 x 33 x 5cm (8½ x 13 x 2in) baking tray (sheet pan), see page 7.

To make the cake, place the chopped apples and plums in a bowl and add the bicarbonate of soda (baking soda) and mix. Set aside.

Cream together the butter and sugar in a large mixing bowl or stand mixer, then add the eggs and vanilla extract and beat until fluffy and light. Now gently fold in the flour and salt, being careful not to over-mix. Next, add the apple and plums, and combine, again being nice and gentle. Pour the mixture into your lined tray and bake for 40-50 minutes.

While the cake is baking, make the topping. Heat all the ingredients together in a heavy-based saucepan over a low heat until the butter melts and the almonds soak up some of the milk. Give it a good stir until it thickens slightly, then set aside.

Check that the cake is ready: you'll know it's done when a knife inserted into the centre comes out cleanish (it's a very pudding-like cake, so don't worry too much if there's a bit of mixture stuck on there). Pour the topping over the cooked cake and spread it out evenly with a spatula, then return to the oven for a further 20 minutes until the top becomes golden brown. It'll be crunchy when it cools.

Best served warm with clotted cream, but still delicious cold with a cup of tea.

This will keep for a week in an airtight container in the fridge.

Other variations could include pineapple or mashed banana;
it's just important to get the moisture balance on the same
level. Other nuts can be used for the topping, but will
probably need breaking up into smaller pieces.

PEANUT COOKIE SLICE

This is one for the peanut fiends, the addicts who need their smooth and crunchy fix and can be caught, spoon in hand, eating straight from the jar. Baking the cookie dough for longer than usual gives it a pleasant chewiness that contrasts perfectly with the peanut and caramel topping.

TO MAKE THE COOKIE BASE

250g (9oz) butter
200g (7oz) caster (superfine) sugar
200g (7oz) soft light brown sugar
200g (7oz) smooth peanut butter
3 medium eggs
400g (14oz) self-raising flour
a pinch of salt

TO MAKE THE PEANUT CARAMEL

50g (1¾oz) butter
150g (5¼oz) caster sugar
150g (5¼oz) golden syrup
300g (10½oz) salted peanuts

Preheat the oven to 160°C fan/320°F/gas 4 and line your 22 x 33 x 5cm (8½ x 13 x 2in) baking tray (sheet pan), see page 7.

To make the cookie base, start by melting the butter in a heavy-based saucepan over a low heat. Once melted, pour it into a mixing bowl and add both sugars. Stir until they start to dissolve, then add the peanut butter and continue mixing until things lighten up. Add the eggs and combine, then gently mix in the flour and salt. Scrape down the sides of the mixing bowl and give everything a short final mix. Transfer the cookie dough to your tray and press it down evenly using your hands or a spatula to make it level. Bake for 35–40 minutes, or until the surface becomes a little darker than is comfortable.

While the cookie base bakes, make the peanut caramel. In a heavy-based saucepan over a medium heat, mix together the butter, sugar and syrup and bring to a gentle boil, stirring the whole time. Keep boiling until the creamy foam starts turning a deep caramel colour. Once that colour appears, add the peanuts to the pan and give it a good mix, then set aside while the cookie finishes baking. Just before the cookie comes out of the oven, put the pan back on the heat and bring the nuts back to the boil, then pour the sticky mixture over the top of the cookie base and spread evenly with a spatula.

Let it all cool down for a while before removing from the tray and cutting into slices.

This will keep for a week in an airtight container in the fridge.

Once it's fully cooled, a drizzle of melted dark or white chocolate on top can take this into a parallel universe.

SOUR CHERRY &
PECAN BLONDIE

If you're looking for that gooey feeling you get when you break open a warm cookie, revealing the soft doughy goodness inside, you can't go wrong with this one. Marry that with a whip crack of sour cherry and crunchy pecans and you may need a safe word to stop you scoffing the lot. If you can't find fresh sour cherries, it's easy enough to rehydrate dried ones in some water.

350g (12oz) butter
150g (5¼oz) pecans, roughly chopped
150g (5¼oz) sour cherries, or 75g (2½oz) dried sour cherries soaked in 125ml (4¼fl oz) boiling water for an hour
1 tablespoon cornflour (cornstarch)
350g (12oz) soft light brown sugar
5 medium eggs
450g (1lb) plain (all-purpose) flour
1 teaspoon baking powder
1 teaspoon salt
300g (10½oz) white chocolate, roughly chopped
sea salt flakes, to top

Preheat the oven to 180°C fan/350°F/gas 6 and line your 22 x 33 x 5cm (8½ x 13 x 2in) baking tray (sheet pan), see page 7.

Melt the butter in a heavy-based pan over a low to medium-low heat. Allow it to start foaming, but stare down any burning: you just want a slight nutty colour and flavour. Tip into a mixing bowl and leave to cool a little. Using the same pan, lightly toast your pecans, so they get a little colour, then set aside.

Now pit your cherries by digging your thumbs into them and pulling the flesh apart, discarding the stones; do this over a large bowl so you don't lose any juice. Things will probably get a little messy, but that's OK. Chop the cherries into a mixture of halves and quarters. Cover with the cornflour (cornstarch) to soak up some of the juice and set aside. Do the same if using dried cherries.

Now beat the sugar into the melted butter, helping it to cool a little more, then add the eggs and beat until emulsified. Add the flour, baking powder and salt and mix lightly, then gently stir in the pecans, white chocolate and finally the cherries, trying not to break them up too much.

Transfer the mixture to your baking tray and spread it out so it's level. Bake for 30 minutes: you want this cake to be slightly underbaked so it has that chewiness in the middle, with a slight cakey-ness on top. To achieve this, you can try the technique of placing the baking tray containing the hot cake tray in a bigger tray filled with iced water as soon as it comes out of the oven: this stops it from continuing to bake in the residual heat, ensuring you get that extra-gooey centre. You can achieve the same thing by popping it in the freezer straight from the oven.

These will keep for a week in an airtight container in the fridge.

Blondies will always deliver a very sweet treat. Calming the sweetness with some miso or warm spice will make this more alluring to the adult palate.

BEETROOT, ROSE & APPLE CAKE

A brilliantly flamboyant pink cake, but without any fake food colouring. The trick when baking with rose water is to use it sparingly. It needs to be a very subtle, almost inaudible backing vocal, bringing just a whisper of harmony. Using Niki Segnit's *The Flavour Thesaurus*, we discovered the trinity of hazelnut, apple and rose. We know it's not everyone's cup of tea, so if you have an aversion to rose, orange blossom is a great alternative. Other fresh or dried flowers look great when decorating, too.

TO MAKE THE CAKE

300g/10½oz beetroots (beets), trimmed and peeled
185g (6½oz) caster (superfine) sugar
185ml (6¼fl oz) / (165g/5¾oz) rapeseed (canola) oil
5 medium eggs
120g (4oz) hazelnut flour
360g (12¾oz) plain (all-purpose) flour
1 teaspoon salt
1 teaspoon bicarbonate of soda (baking soda)
1 teaspoon baking powder
350g (12oz) peeled, cored and chopped apple (about 3 apples)
1 teaspoon rose water

TO MAKE THE ICING

15ml (1 tablespoon) beetroot juice
2 teaspoons lemon juice
1 teaspoon rose water
250g (9oz) icing (confectioners') sugar, sifted
3g dried rose petals (optional)

Pictured on page 113.

Preheat the oven to 160°C fan/320°F/gas 4 and line your 22 x 33 x 5cm (8½ x 13 x 2in) baking tray (sheet pan), see page 7.

Grate the beetroots (beets): you should get about 215g (7½oz) grated flesh. Place this in a sieve over a bowl, with a weight on top of the grated beetroot to help drain the juice. You'll need about 15ml (1 tablespoon), so the grated mass will reduce to about 200g (7oz) with the loss of the juice.

Combine the sugar and oil in a large mixing bowl or stand mixer, then add the eggs and emulsify until the mixture looks glossy. Add the hazelnut flour, then sift in the plain (all-purpose) flour, salt, bicarbonate of soda (baking soda) and baking powder and lightly combine. Finally, add the drained grated beetroot, chopped apples and rose water, keeping the drained beetroot juice aside for the icing. Pour the cake mixture into your lined tray and bake for 40 minutes.

Meanwhile, make the icing by mixing together the beetroot juice, lemon juice, rose water and icing (confectioners') sugar in a large bowl until well combined. When the cake comes out of the oven and is still warm in the tray, drizzle the icing over the top, and sprinkle with some dried rose petals if you have any. The icing will be rather wet, but don't worry: this helps it soak into the cake crumb. Leave to cool.

This will keep for 4 days in an airtight container in the fridge.

If you're using orange blossom water or orange extract, try using some candied orange peel (see page 156 to make your own) instead of the flower petals: it will taste good and give a contrasting and distinguished look.

HEDGEROW CAKE

Somehow, the British hedgerow can make you feel cosy. Even when we're outdoors in the middle of winter, it shelters us from high winds and rain. Translating the hedgerow into a cake leads straight to blackberries, with their earthy undertones and herbaceous high notes. The upfront acidity and vibrant colour are the obvious star qualities of this fruit, and they're combined with toasted hazelnuts for a warm woodiness that brings this cake to life. Late-fruiting raspberries can be a nice addition, too. You could also try swapping out a little of the plain (all-purpose) flour for wholemeal (wholewheat) with the nuttiness of the bran.

TO MAKE THE CAKE

5 medium eggs
250g (9oz) caster
  (superfine) sugar
200ml (7fl oz) / (180g/6⅓oz)
  rapeseed (canola) oil
150g (5¼oz) hazelnut flour
300g (10½oz) plain
  (all-purpose) flour
2 teaspoons baking powder
½ teaspoon salt
2 apples (200g/7oz of flesh)
2 pears (200g/7oz of flesh)
300g (10½oz) blackberries (other
  soft berries, like blackcurrants and
  raspberries, can be used too)

TO MAKE THE ICING

220g (7¾oz) icing
  (confectioners') sugar
50g (1¾oz) blackberries

TO MAKE THE NUT TOPPING

50g (1¾oz) whole hazelnuts,
  blanched if possible

Pictured on page 112.

Preheat the oven to 160°C fan/320°F/gas 4 and line your 22 x 33 x 5cm (8½ x 13 x 2in) baking tray (sheet pan), see page 7.

To make the cake, combine the eggs and sugar in a large mixing bowl or stand mixer and mix well to form an emulsion. While mixing, add the oil slowly, so the mix doesn't split. Add the hazelnut flour and then sift in the plain (all-purpose) flour, baking powder and salt, and give everything a light mix.

Next, take one apple and one pear and grate them with the skin on, then peel the other apple and pear and chop both into small chunks a little bigger than a pea. Add the grated and chopped apples and pears to the cake mix, along with the berries, and stir. As you mix them in, you want the berries to break up slightly, but not so much that they lose their integrity, so go gently.

Pour into your lined tray and bake for 50–60 minutes until the top is golden brown. More importantly, the centre needs to be cooked, as there's a lot of moisture in this cake, so check by sticking a knife into the middle: it should come out clean.

To make the icing, sift the icing (confectioners') sugar into a large bowl, then press the blackberries through a sieve into the bowl; this will remove the seeds and create a pulp. You can use the back of a spoon to push them through. Remember to scrape the bottom of the sieve, as this is where most of the pulp will gather. Keep pressing the seeds and scraping underneath to get the most out of the berries, then mix the pulp into the icing sugar. The mixture might be a little stiff, so add a splash of water or lemon juice to loosen things up if necessary, or use a bit more fruit pulp if you have any spare berries.

Leave the cake to fully cool in the tray, then transfer to a chopping board and spread the icing over the top.

If you don't have blanched hazelnuts, you can toast the hazelnuts for the topping and remove the husks by rubbing them in a dish towel (see page 43). Once this is done, simply smash up the nuts and sprinkle over the icing while it's still a little wet and sticky. If you're using blanched, just skip straight to smashing and sprinkling.

This will keep for 5 days in an airtight container in the fridge.

PEAR & WALNUT CAKE

Finding a perfectly ripe pear is like winning the lottery these days. Unripe pears will sit in a fruit bowl for weeks, never becoming soft, just withering away into some kind of limbo between the fruit bowl and the compost bin. Fear not, though, this cake is designed with exactly these pears in mind. They work really well in this recipe, with their firmness diminishing in the heat of the oven to give the perfect balanced texture.

4 pears (roughly 500g/1lb 2oz)
100g (3½oz) caster
 (superfine) sugar
250g (9oz) soft butter
250g (9oz) soft light brown sugar
5 medium eggs
250g (9oz) wholemeal
 (wholewheat) flour
1½ teaspoons baking powder
50g (1¾oz) hazelnut flour
50g (1¾oz) walnut pieces
1 tablespoon golden syrup
 or honey

Preheat the oven to 160°C fan/320°F/gas 4 and line your 22 x 33 x 5cm (8½ x 13 x 2in) baking tray (sheet pan), see page 7.

Slice the pears into thin wedges. Depending on the size or ripeness of your pears, you may need to remove pips.

Place the pears in a bowl with the caster (superfine) sugar and toss them with a light vigour until they are fully coated, then set aside.

In a large mixing bowl or stand mixer, cream the butter and soft light brown sugar until fluffy, then add the eggs and beat until fully emulsified. Now add the wholemeal (wholewheat) flour, baking powder and hazelnut flour, and fold until you have a smooth batter. Scrape down the sides of the bowl and give it one final mix, then pour the batter into your lined tray. Level the top using a spatula, then arrange the pears on top, spacing them out evenly. Pour over any liquid that has leached from the pears, then scatter over the walnuts. Drizzle the golden syrup or honey over the cake, giving the walnuts the majority of the attention. Bake for 40–50 minutes until the top turns golden brown and the slices of pear begin to crisp. Leave to cool in the tray before transferring to a chopping board to slice.

This will keep for 5 days in an airtight container in the fridge.

This recipe will work with apples too. For a lighter cake, white flour can give more lift, but this will cause more of the pear slices to sink into the batter; this isn't a bad thing, though, as it will create little pockets of pear in a thirsty crumb.

MERINGUE CAKE

Ideally, you want some sour fruit in the centre of this cake to punch through the meringue and hit you in the face, remedying the sweetness. It's similar to a Louise cake, which uses a layer of jam in the middle. You could try that, or even some sort of curd, perhaps passion fruit or sea buckthorn. We've found the frozen bags of mixed summer fruits are pretty good for this recipe, and you can top the sponge mixture with them while they're still frozen. But obviously, fresh fruits are really good too.

TO MAKE THE CAKE

150g (5¼oz) soft butter
125g (4¼oz) caster
  (superfine) sugar
4 medium egg yolks
100g (3½oz) plain yoghurt
finely grated zest of 1 lemon
  and juice of ½
150g (5¼oz) plain
  (all-purpose) flour
a pinch of salt
1 teaspoon baking powder
500g (1lb 2oz) summer fruits
  (blackcurrants, red currants,
  raspberries, blackberries)
1 tablespoon cornflour (cornstarch)

TO MAKE THE MERINGUE

4 medium egg whites
200g (7oz) caster sugar
a pinch of salt
juice of ½ lemon
1 tablespoon cornflour

NUT FREE

Preheat the oven to 180°C fan/350°F/gas 6 and line your 22 x 33 x 5cm (8½ x 13 x 2in) baking tray (sheet pan), see page 7.

To make the cake, cream the butter and sugar in a large bowl or stand mixer until light and fluffy, then beat in the egg yolks and stir in the yoghurt and lemon zest. Sift in the flour, salt and baking powder, then fold in until combined. Spread the mixture across the base of your lined tray, being careful to get full and even coverage.

Put the fruit in a bowl with the lemon juice and cornflour (cornstarch) and stir to combine. Now arrange the fruit on top of the cake batter, cutting any large pieces in half. Avoid dumping too much fruit in the middle, as that's the last place the sponge will cook; it's best to distribute more around the edges. Bake for 30 minutes until the sponge puffs up around the pieces of fruit and begins to turn golden brown.

Meanwhile, to make the meringue, beat together the egg whites and sugar in a clean bowl for 5–6 minutes until the mixture starts looking like white emulsion paint. Add the other ingredients and mix for a further minute or so until thick and glossy.

When the fruit and sponge layer is ready, spread the meringue over the top, making small peaks with the back of a spoon. Reduce the oven temperature to 160°C fan/320°F/gas 4 and bake for another 25 minutes until the meringue is firm and browning at the peaks. Leave to cool in the tray for half an hour before transferring to a chopping board.

This will keep for 4 days in an airtight container in the fridge.

Gooseberries work really well in this cake, too. Just be sure to cut them up into small pieces first.

HONEY, LEMON & GINGER CHEESECAKE

This is a belter of a cheesecake. However, it's a bit like Marmite, in that most people go crazy for it but some detest it. If you love ginger and honey, then go for it. This does grow on people, too: it may be an acquired taste initially, but you'll soon have them eating out of the palm of your hand. If you feel noncommittal towards the ginger, then just leave it out. A honey-flavoured cheesecake is still seriously delicious.

TO MAKE THE BASE

125g (4¼oz) butter
200g (7oz) soft light brown sugar
1 medium egg
100g (3½oz) plain
  (all-purpose) flour
2 teaspoons ground ginger
a pinch of salt

TO MAKE THE FILLING

800g (1lb 12oz) cream cheese
250g (9oz) honey
6 medium eggs
50ml (1¾fl oz) lemon juice
  (1 juicy lemon)
3 tablespoons cornflour
  (cornstarch)

TO TOP

50g (1¾oz) stem (preserved)
  ginger
50g (1¾oz) stem ginger syrup
  (from the jar) or honey
15g (⅔oz) bee pollen
  (or crushed-up ginger nuts/
  ginger snaps or chunks of
  honeycomb)

Preheat the oven to 180°C fan/350°F/gas 6 and line your 22 x 33 x 5cm (8½ x 13 x 2in) baking tray (sheet pan), see page 7.

Take your cream cheese out of the fridge as it needs to be at room temperature for the filling.

You can make the base by hand or using a stand mixer; either works well. Start by melting the butter in a heavy-based saucepan over a low heat, then transfer it to a mixing bowl. Add the sugar and beat until well combined, then add the egg and mix it all together. Sift in the flour, ground ginger and salt and fold until you have a smooth batter. Spread this into your lined tray using a spatula, making sure to get an even spread across the tray and right into the corners. Bake for around 25 minutes, or until dark golden. It might rise up at the edges in places, but that's OK: it creates a really nice crispy edge and helps to cradle the cheesecake filling.

To make the filling, whip the cream cheese in a large mixing bowl or your stand mixer until smooth, then add the honey until combined. Add the eggs and mix slowly until you have a nicely emulsified mixture. Pour in the lemon juice and combine, then mix in the cornflour (cornstarch) until you have a nice lump-free mixture.

Now pour the cream cheese mixture over the top of the baked base and return to the oven for 35 minutes, or until you have a smooth, set top. Cracks can appear if it's overbaked, so try to be brave when taking it out and keep a little jiggle in the middle. Another way to bake cheesecake is by sitting your tray in an even larger tray filled with water, so the water comes about halfway up. Baking a cheesecake in this fashion will take a little longer, but it does tend to crack less often with this method.

While the cheesecake is baking, prepare the topping by blending the stem (preserved) ginger and syrup or honey in a blender to make a paste. When the cheesecake comes out of the oven, brush this paste over the top, then sprinkle over the bee pollen for decoration and texture. Nature's hundreds and thousands!

Best eaten chilled. This will keep for 5 days in an airtight container in the fridge.

SEA BUCKTHORN CHEESECAKE

Sea buckthorn has been stepping out of its wild and thorny thickets into the limelight recently, and rightly so. It's got an incredible flavour that's half Solero sunshine and half screw-your-face-up sharpness. It's a rare berry that's native to the UK. You can get sea buckthorn from various health-food shops as dried berries or juice, or order frozen berries online. This recipe incorporates it with just the right level of sweetness through the cheesecake mixture, and the bright orange topping gives it that vibrant panache that really turns heads.

TO MAKE THE BASE

40g (1½oz) buckwheat groats
125g (4¼oz) soft butter
250g (9oz) caster
 (superfine) sugar
1 medium egg
60g (2oz) plain (all-purpose) flour

TO MAKE THE CAKE

680g (1lb 8oz) cream cheese
250g (9oz) caster sugar
40ml (1½fl oz) lemon juice
 (about 1 lemon)
6 medium eggs
200ml (7fl oz) sea buckthorn purée
 (see note)
60g (2oz) plain flour
a pinch of salt

TO MAKE THE TOPPING

3 sheets of gelatine
250ml (8½fl oz) sea buckthorn
 purée (see note)
50g (1¾oz) caster sugar

NUT FREE

Preheat the oven to 180°C fan/350°F/gas 6 and line your 22 x 33 x 5cm (8½ x 13 x 2in) baking tray (sheet pan), see page 7.

To make the cheesecake base, begin by toasting the buckwheat groats in a dry pan over a medium heat until they start to smell nutty and look nicely caramelized. Take off the heat and allow to cool a little, then blitz them in a spice grinder or blender so they break up a bit.

Mix the butter, sugar and egg together in a large mixing bowl or stand mixer until well combined, then add the flour and buckwheat. Combine well, then use a spatula to evenly spread the mixture into your lined tray, right into the corners. Bake for 20–25 minutes until golden brown.

Meanwhile, make the filling. Put the cream cheese in a large mixing bowl or using a stand mixer with a paddle attachment, mix for about a minute until it's nice and smooth. Add the sugar and lemon juice and continue to mix, then mix in the eggs. Give the sides of the bowl a good scrape down and add the sea buckthorn purée while mixing slowly. Finally, sift in the flour and salt a little at a time, and keep mixing until the flour is well combined and there are no lumps.

When the base is ready, pour the filling mixture over the top and return to the oven for another 30–35 minutes.

Meanwhile, make the topping. Soak the gelatine sheets in a bowl of cold water for 5 minutes, then wring out any excess water. In a heavy-based pan over a low heat, combine the sea buckthorn purée with the sugar and stir to dissolve, then add the gelatine sheets and warm together. Be careful not to boil it; you just want to dissolve the gelatine and sugar. Once it's ready, take it off the heat.

When the cheesecake is out of the oven, pour the topping over – you might need to tilt the baking tray to get an even layer. Leave to set overnight and serve cold. Slice this cake when chilled, with a thin, sharp knife, to give a really clean-cut look.

This will keep for 5 days in an airtight container in the fridge.

You can make your own sea buckthorn purée using the berries. Heat 600g (1lb 5oz) berries in a heavy-based saucepan over a medium heat until they soften and break down, then whizz them up in a blender until smooth. Pass through a sieve, press all the liquid out of the pulp with the back of a spoon. Discard the pulp.

A TRIFLE BIZARRE

It's easy to get in a pickle with this trifle. The elements are all simple enough – it's the timings that might catch you out. We find it useful to think about it as building tasty layers of time, so you'll need a solid plan and a clear schedule for this one. This is a trifle with a clean look, as if it were a naturally occurring rock structure with a perfectly layered stratum of sponge, jelly, custard and cream, mined from the trifle quarry and chiselled into a monolithic party piece. It still brings all the fun of a trifle, just less of the mess. This recipe uses half a batch of the Sponge Cake batter from the Basic Bakes chapter (pages 18–45), so just halve the quantities and mix as directed.

In order to capture the true British style of trifle, we've used custard powder and shop-bought jelly (jello). However, if you're feeling ambitious and want to get creative, you can make your own custard and infuse it with different flavours for different seasons. Match the jelly to it, or even make your own fruit juice and set it with gelatine. Splash some booze on the sponge or fold it through the cream for the more grown-up party.

TO MAKE THE SPONGE
half a batch of Sponge Cake batter
(page 24)

TO MAKE THE JELLY
2 x 135g (4¾oz) packs of
shop-bought strawberry jelly
(jello)
390ml (13¼fl oz) boiling water
390ml (13¼fl oz) cold water
400g (14oz) fresh strawberries,
sliced into 3mm (⅛in) slices

TO MAKE THE CUSTARD
70g (2½oz) custard powder
(we use Bird's)
30g (1oz) caster (superfine) sugar
570ml (19¼fl oz) whole milk

TO MAKE THE CREAM
100g (3½oz) icing
(confectioners') sugar
400g (14oz) double (heavy) cream
250g (9oz) mascarpone
1 teaspoon vanilla paste

TO TOP
hundreds and thousands, chocolate
shavings or popping candy

Pictured on page 11.

Preheat the oven to 160°C fan/320°F/gas 4 and line your 22 x 33 x 5cm (8½ x 13 x 2in) baking tray (sheet pan), see page 7.

Spread the sponge batter across the base of your lined tray using a spatula, making sure you get a nice, even layer. Bake for 40–45 minutes: this is a little longer than you'd bake it for normally, but it needs to toughen up, ready for holding the jelly. Once it comes out of the oven, get it straight in the fridge to chill.

Meanwhile, make the jelly. Cut the shop-bought jelly (jello) into cubes and place in a large bowl. Pour over the boiling water and whisk together until all the cubes have dissolved, then add the cold water and continue whisking until the mixture is well combined and there are no tiny lumps left at all. Place in the fridge for around 15 minutes to cool.

Arrange the sliced strawberries over the cooled sponge in the tray, trying not to overlap them, but covering as much of the sponge as possible. Once the jelly liquid is fully cold, pour it gently over the sponge and strawberries, trying not to move them around too much. Lots of the jelly will soak into the sponge, but that's OK; it will also rise and cover the strawberries. Carefully transfer the tray to the fridge, making sure that it is completely level (you might need to prop it up slightly at one end or another like I do, as my fridge is definitely not level).

Leave in the fridge for 1 hour to completely firm up.

Meanwhile, it's time to make the custard. Place the custard powder and sugar in a heavy-based saucepan and use a whisk to mix together. Pour in a splash of the milk and whisk until a smooth paste forms; it's important to get this smooth so you don't end up with lumpy custard. Place the saucepan over a medium heat and pour in the rest of the milk, whisking all the while. The mixture will start to thicken as it reaches a soft boil. Once it's thick and smooth, remove from the heat and continue stirring to let some of the heat out, then transfer the custard to a bowl and place a piece of cling film (plastic wrap) directly on top of the custard – you want it to be touching the surface, all the way to the edges. This will stop the custard from forming a skin. Pop the bowl in the fridge for around 30 minutes.

While everything else is chilling, make the cream topping. You'll need two bowls for this. Sift the icing (confectioners') sugar into one, then add the double (heavy) cream and whisk until you have stiff peaks. Add the mascarpone and vanilla to another bowl and beat together until light and smooth. Now fold the two together until well combined, and put this in the fridge.

Once the custard has been in the fridge for 30 minutes, take it out and remove the cling film. It will still be a little warm, and could have formed a few lumps as it has started to set; you can get rid of these by whisking until it's smooth again. Take the sponge out of the fridge and check that the jelly has set with the strawberries in place. Dollop the custard evenly on top, then gently spread it across the strawberries using a spatula until you have an even layer. Put the tray back in the fridge for another 30 minutes to let the custard fully set, then top with the cream mixture, again trying to get it as even as possible, with a nice, smooth top. A palette knife is good for this.

Sprinkle the trifle with the topping of your choice, then leave to set for at least another hour before serving chilled. Make sure to cut this with a super-sharp knife and wipe the blade between cuts; that way, you'll get a crisp view of all the colourful layers.

Best eaten chilled. This will keep for 3 days in an airtight container in the fridge.

Make sure you have enough fridge space before you start, as the different elements need to cool separately.

A great variation on this recipe is to turn it into a Black Forest gâteau trifle. Douse the sponge in kirsch, use fresh cherries instead of strawberries and a chocolate crème pat instead of custard, then finish with dark chocolate shavings on top.

WHOLESOME

After all the gluttony of the previous chapters, you may fancy a purge, so what better way to cleanse your soul than by delving into this worthy pool of wholesome recipes?

Making use of heritage grains, sugar alternatives and healthier nuts or seeds can give you a more health-conscious repertoire, without compromising on flavour, texture or even aesthetic. This section is a nod to the Californian health movement, with its roots firmly planted in sixties and seventies alternative culture. The food that sprung from that movement wasn't just about health for our bodies; it was a part of something bigger. It was about free thinking and environmental protection, a reaction to the socially prescribed mass production of processed foods that was starting to infiltrate daily life. Recipes like these are linked to that time, and now more than ever, it's important to stay attached to the reality that the food we make and buy directly affects the environment that sustains us, and that cooking together creates community, creativity and peace. So keep it local, put a flower in your hair and share the love through cake.

SESAME & HONEY BARS

This is like a soft, cakey version of those packets of sesame brittles often bought by parents as a so-called healthy snack for their kids. There is some serious sweetness going on here, but, like a treacle tart, sometimes the wonder of baking just delivers.

TO MAKE THE PASTRY BASE

225g (8oz) soft butter
250g (9oz) honey
 (local, if possible)
250g (9oz) spelt flour
 (if you can get hold of locally
 grown wholemeal/wholewheat,
 then all the better)

TO MAKE THE TOPPING

6 medium eggs, beaten
360g (12¾oz) honey
100g (3½oz) desiccated (dried
 shredded) coconut
150g (5¼oz) sesame seeds
1 teaspoon baking powder

Preheat the oven to 180°C fan/350°F/gas 6 and line your 22 x 33 x 5cm (8½ x 13 x 2in) baking tray (sheet pan), see page 7.

To make the pastry base, add all the ingredients to a large bowl and mix until well combined. Spread this into your lined tray using a spatula, making sure to get a nice, even layer across the base of the tray. Bake for 15–20 minutes, or until lightly golden.

Meanwhile, in a large mixing bowl, beat together the eggs and honey, then gently fold in the coconut, sesame seeds and baking powder.

When the pastry base comes out of the oven, pour the topping over it and return to the oven for a further 20–25 minutes, or until golden and slightly domed at the edges.

This will keep for 2 weeks in an airtight container in the fridge.

This is a very sweet cake, so it's best to cut into smaller slices. They'll still pack a pretty hefty honey punch. You could also add some lemon zest or mixed peel to contrast the sweetness if you like.

APRICOT & WHITE CHOCOLATE FLAPJACK

If you have a busy lifestyle and don't have time to watch apricots ripen on the tree, but still want to make homemade cakes, then dried fruit is your friend. Dried apricots may not have the romance of the fresh, plump variety, but they still hold a whole load of flavour. Or for a super-simple version of this, you can just use shop-bought apricot jam instead of making your own purée. If you're not worried about keeping it vegan, some yoghurt icing will add a bit more tartness.

TO MAKE THE APRICOT PURÉE
290g (10¼oz) dried apricots, chopped
290ml (9¾fl oz) water

TO MAKE THE FLAPJACK
310g (11oz) chopped pecans
480g (1lb 1oz) gluten-free oats (ideally a mixture of jumbo and rolled)
1 teaspoon salt
260g (9¼oz) golden syrup
200g (7oz) coconut oil
200g (7oz) soft light brown sugar

TO MAKE THE TOPPING
65g (2¼oz) vegan white chocolate (or just regular white chocolate if you're not worried about keeping it vegan)

A piping bag is useful for this recipe, but is not essential

VEGAN
GLUTEN FREE

Preheat the oven to 180°C fan/350°F/gas 6 and line your 22 x 33 x 5cm (8½ x 13 x 2in) baking tray (sheet pan), see page 7.

Begin by making the apricot purée. Simply combine the dried apricots and water in a heavy-based saucepan over a medium–high heat. Stir occasionally, then simmer for about 15 minutes until the apricots completely relent, becoming soft and absorbing all the water.

Next, crush the pecans to break them up, but not too small. They're not the sturdiest of nuts, so you can just do this by hand over a large bowl, then add the oats and salt and mix thoroughly.

Warm the golden syrup, oil and brown sugar in a heavy-based pan over a medium heat until the sugar has completely dissolved, then pour this mixture over the dry ingredients. Mix everything together really well, making sure there are no dry clumps of oats hiding away.

When you're happy with the consistency, weigh about 900g (2lb) of the flapjack mixture into your lined tray, spreading it out evenly and smoothing it down with a spatula. You want to create a nice, dense base layer here – the best way to do this is to place a sheet of baking parchment over the mixture, then place another baking tray on top and press down.

Now spoon the apricot purée all over the pressed flapjack and spread it out evenly using a spatula. Finally, scatter the remainder of the flapjack mixture over the top and smooth it down gently; you want this top layer to be a bit jagged and not as compressed as the base layer. Bake for 50 minutes until the edges of the flapjack begin to turn golden brown.

Just before the flapjack comes out of the oven, melt the white chocolate in a bain-marie (see page 8), then pop it into a piping bag. Snip a piping hole about 3mm (⅛in) thick in the end of the bag, then pipe the white chocolate over the flapjack in a diagonal motion and leave to cool in the fridge in the tray. If you don't have a piping bag, it's not a problem. Just use a spoon or fork to trickle or flick the chocolate over the flapjack.

Allow to come up to room temperature before eating. These will keep for 2 weeks in an airtight container in the fridge.

DARK & SEEDY FLAPJACK

This twisted flapjack perverts the rules of flavour, with a complete disregard for any delicate palates out there. It's full-on and makes no apologies for it, hitting your taste buds with maximum levels of molasses and caramelized sugar notes. If you're a fan of the darker things in life – black coffee, espresso, or anything with that shady, treacly goodness – then this is for you. The seeds give it the complexity it needs and help to cut through the stickiness, and it has a crunchy-on-the-outside, sticky-in-the-middle texture, perfect for sharing at a clandestine meeting over a cup of something sinister.

600g (1lb 5oz) gluten-free oats (a mixture of jumbo and porridge/rolled is good)
250g (9oz) mixed seeds (such as sunflower, pumpkin, flax, sesame, chia and poppy – see notes)
1 teaspoon ground mixed (pumpkin pie) spice
1 teaspoon salt
375g (13¼oz) butter
185g (6½oz) golden syrup
130g (4½oz) black treacle (molasses)
210g (7½oz) soft light brown sugar

GLUTEN FREE

Preheat the oven to 180°C fan/350°F/gas 6 and line your 22 x 33 x 5cm (8½ x 13 x 2in) baking tray (sheet pan), see page 7.

In a large bowl, thoroughly mix together the oats, seeds, mixed (pumpkin pie) spice and salt.

Next, pop the butter, golden syrup, treacle and brown sugar in a heavy-based saucepan over a medium heat and stir until the sugar has dissolved and the butter is fully melted. Pour this buttery syrup over your dry ingredients and mix thoroughly with a spoon. Plonk the mixture into your lined tray and smooth down with the back of a spoon or spatula so that it's flat and even. Bake for 30–40 minutes until the top is a deep-brown colour. All the foaming butter will eventually disappear as it cooks, and the middle of the flapjack should still be soft with a little movement to it as it comes out of the oven.

Leave to cool completely in the tray before cutting.

This will keep for a few weeks when stored in an airtight container in the fridge.

This flapjack will still be standing shoulder to shoulder with the cockroaches after the nuclear fall-out, but if you feel it needs using up, try breaking it into pieces in a bowl and pouring over milk for a serious cereal snack.

It's best to use larger quantities of the bigger seeds, like pumpkin and sunflower. Poppy and chia seeds can really get all up in your gums and teeth, so it's best to not have these as the headliners.

RAMBLEJACK

Growing up in the eighties, health-food shops were rife with giant slabs of dry, joyless flapjacks that crumbled to dust in your hands. We wanted to update that version from our childhoods, and a date slice is a stone-cold classic, so we kept all the best bits and added a little flair and stability, upping the sweetness a tiny bit and making the dates into a jam instead of a stew, then topping it off with chocolate. A big upgrade, but still a nostalgic throwback for anyone craving the old-school health-food feels. Now you can take it out on a ramble without the risk of total collapse.

TO MAKE THE DATE JAM
290g (10¼oz) dried chopped dates
290ml (9¾fl oz) water

TO MAKE THE FLAPJACK
315g (11¼oz) chopped walnuts
480g (1lb 1oz) gluten-free oats
  (a mixture of jumbo and
  porridge/rolled is good)
1 teaspoon salt
260g (9¼oz) golden syrup
200g (7oz) coconut oil
200g (7oz) soft light brown sugar

TO MAKE THE TOPPING
80g (3oz) dark chocolate
1 tablespoon desiccated (dried
  shredded) coconut

A piping bag is good for this,
  but not essential

VEGAN
GLUTEN FREE

Preheat the oven to 180°C fan/350°F/gas 6 and line your 22 x 33 x 5cm (8½ x 13 x 2in) baking tray (sheet pan), see page 7.

To make the date jam, combine the dates and water in a large pan over a medium heat and cook until the dates have softened and broken down to form a soft paste. Set aside.

Blitz your walnuts in a food processor to break them up into a rough rubble, then mix them with the oats and salt in a large bowl.

In a separate pan, warm the golden syrup, oil and brown sugar over a medium heat until the sugar has dissolved and everything is fully combined into a beautiful silky black mass.

Pour this into the bowl with the dry ingredients and mix thoroughly, then weigh 900g (2lb) of the mix into the prepared tray and smooth down. The easiest way to do this is by covering it with a sheet of baking parchment and then pressing it down with the base of another baking tray; you want a nice, even top, so you can press quite hard.

Now add the date jam mixture by spreading it across the pressed oats, making sure to spread it evenly: the back of a metal serving spoon works well, or a spatula. Finally, loosely scatter the remaining flapjack mixture across the top, then gently smooth with a spatula.

Bake this for 45 minutes until golden, then remove from the oven and set aside.

To make the topping, melt the chocolate in a bain-marie (see page 8), then transfer it into a piping bag. Snip a piping hole about 3mm (⅛in) thick in the end of the bag, then pipe the chocolate over the flapjack in a diagonal pattern before sprinkling with the desiccated (dried shredded) coconut. No piping bag? No problem! It's time to pretend you're an artistic genius. Hold your bowl of melted chocolate just above the flapjack and, using a fork, flick torrents of melted chocolate all over the top to finish the masterpiece. The messier, the better.

Leave to cool in the tray. These will keep for 2 weeks in an airtight container in the fridge.

BIRD FOOD COOKIE SLICE

These cookie slices look a bit like a rectangular version of the fat balls you find hanging around suburban gardens for all the birds to peck at. Hopefully, though, these taste a lot better. This is a variation on our seedy flapjack, but in cookie form. It's worth trying this recipe with agave syrup, or if that doesn't suit your taste, try some good old golden syrup instead; just remember to warm it up before mixing with the seeds, so it becomes nice and runny. This recipe only uses a food processor – no stand mixer required – but you can make it by hand if you don't have one.

TO MAKE THE COOKIE LAYER

200g (7oz) oatmeal
200g (7oz) wholemeal
  (wholewheat) flour
1 teaspoon baking powder
250g (9oz) coconut oil
150g (5¼oz) soft light brown sugar
100g (3½oz) caster
  (superfine) sugar
200g (7oz) maple syrup
a pinch of salt

TO MAKE THE SEED LAYER

300g (10½oz) mixed seeds
  (we suggest: 150g/5¼oz pumpkin
  seeds, 100g/3½oz sunflower
  seeds and 50g/1¾oz flax, but you
  can use whatever mix you like)
100g (3½oz) maple syrup
a pinch of salt

VEGAN

Preheat the oven to 160°C fan/320°F/gas 4 and line your 22 x 33 x 5cm (8½ x 13 x 2in) baking tray (sheet pan), see page 7.

To make the cookie layer, place the oatmeal, flour, baking powder and coconut oil in a food processor and pulse to combine. Add the sugars, maple syrup and a pinch of salt and blitz a little more until fully combined, then, with damp palms or a spatula, press the mixture into your lined tray.

Now to make the seed layer, mix together the seeds and maple syrup in a bowl with a pinch of salt and stir so the seeds are coated. Spread them on top of the cookie mixture and gently press them in a little.

Bake for 25–30 minutes until the edges of the cookie base turn golden brown; you'll see these bits in the corners. Allow to cool in the tray for a while to firm up before cutting.

This will keep for a week in an airtight container in the fridge.

If you don't have oatmeal, then just put some oats in a food processor and whizz them up: boom, oatmeal.

FRUIT CAKE

A little bit of planning is required for this one, due to the need to soak the fruit overnight. The resulting cake has a light softness to it that makes it more like a vegan version of a Dundee cake than the traditional dark matter served up by your Aunt Doris on a Sunday afternoon. If you're feeling even more fruity, then add a glug of whisky into the mix.

900g (2lb) dried fruit
(a mix of figs, apricots, chopped
dates, sultanas and raisins)
400ml (14fl oz) apple juice
(see notes)
2 ripe bananas (150g/5oz
peeled weight)
130g (4½oz) soft brown sugar
300ml (10fl oz) 270g (9½oz)
sunflower oil, or any neutral oil
250g (9oz) wholemeal
(wholewheat) or spelt flour
2 teaspoons baking powder
4 teaspoons ground mixed
(pumpkin pie) spice
a pinch of salt

VEGAN

Pictured on page 135.

Put all the dried fruit in a bowl; if your dried apricots are whole, roughly chop them first. Pour over the apple juice and leave to soak overnight.

The next day, preheat the oven to 160°C fan/320°F/gas 4 and line your 22 x 33 x 5cm (8½ x 13 x 2in) baking tray (sheet pan), see page 7.

Beat the ripe bananas and sugar in a large mixing bowl or stand mixer until they're emulsified and glossy. Then, while mixing briskly, slowly pour in the oil. Fold in the remaining ingredients, including the fruit and juice from last night's sleepover, until fully combined.

Turn out the mix into your lined tray, then cover with foil: this will ensure the fruit doesn't burn, and will also create a kind of steam chamber as it bakes. Bake for 1 hour, then remove the foil to allow the cake to brown a little on top and bake for a further 15 minutes. Check the cake is cooked by stabbing the centre with a knife; it should come out clean. Leave to cool in the tray.

Best eaten while still slightly warm or at room temperature. This will keep for 2 weeks in an airtight container in the fridge.

This feels like a bit of a worthy cake, so you might assume using local, single-variety, freshly pressed apple juice is essential - but actually, a carton of concentrated apple juice is also fine.

If you wish to decorate, allow the cake to cool beforehand. We'd recommend using our vegan Cashew Frosting recipe (if you aren't avoiding nuts, see page 142), and topping with sliced fresh figs for colour. It's also delicious naked.

SPELT BANANA BREAD

Spelt and banana go hand in hand, each somehow creating the perfect environment for the other to shine, and this banana bread is a booming showcase for that. It's a pretty classic recipe, really, one that you can smash out again and again and never get bored of scoffing. Make sure the bananas used for this cake are large and very soft, otherwise you'll have a dry cake, and we'll be having words. The riper, the better. Buy them in advance if you need to, or whenever you spy an old, blackened banana alone in the fruit bowl, peel it and pop in the freezer until you save up enough to make this cake.

TO MAKE THE BANANA BREAD

5 large, riper-than-ripe bananas
   (700g/1lb 9oz peeled weight)
300g (10½oz) soft butter
350g (12oz) caster
   (superfine) sugar
5 medium eggs
400g (14oz) wholemeal
   (wholewheat) spelt flour
2 teaspoons baking powder
1 teaspoon salt

TO TOP

2 bananas, thinly sliced lengthways
50g (1¾oz) demerara sugar

NUT FREE

Pictured on page 135.

Preheat the oven to 160°C fan/320°F/gas 4 and line your 22 x 33 x 5cm (8½ x 13 x 2in) baking tray (sheet pan), see page 7.

To make the banana bread, place the bananas and butter in a large mixing bowl or stand mixer and combine well, then add the sugar and eggs and mix until well combined. Scrape down the sides and bottom of the bowl and mix again, then add the flour, baking powder and salt, a little at a time, folding gently until incorporated. Transfer this mixture to your lined tray.

For the topping, lay the long, thin banana slices on top of the batter, then sprinkle over the demerara sugar, paying particular attention to the bananas. Bake for 1 hour, or until a knife inserted into the middle comes out clean. Leave to cool in the tray for 15 minutes before transferring to a chopping board.

Best eaten warm or at room temperature. This will keep for a week in an airtight container in the fridge.

Banana bread is one of those things that, once you have a good recipe, you can really go to town on making it your own. It wouldn't be a crime to sling some chocolate chips in there, or even some toasted walnuts.

DEVON APPLE CAKE

Dorset owns the apple cake, but being Devon-based, we need to fight our corner, so this is a recipe to call our own. To make it a true Devon apple cake, we make it with ingredients from within a 10-mile radius of our bakery, with spices to amplify the flavours. Utilizing the apple in three different ways means you really get the most out of this ingredient: the grated apple binds things and keeps it moist; the cubed apples take on a custardy form when cooked, and the slices on top caramelize with the sugar to bring a *tarte tatin* quality.

TO MAKE THE CAKE
450g (1lb) wholemeal (wholewheat) flour (use spelt or a good heritage grain if you can find it)
2 teaspoons baking powder
1 teaspoon bicarbonate of soda (baking soda)
1 teaspoon ground mixed (pumpkin pie) spice
1 teaspoon ground cinnamon
a pinch of salt
300g (10½oz) soft butter
500g (1lb 2oz) apple flesh (about 5 apples)
300g (10½oz) honey
3 medium eggs, beaten

TO TOP
300g (10½oz) apple flesh (about 3 apples)
50g (1¾oz) demerara sugar
2 pinches of ground cinnamon

NUT FREE

Pictured on page 134.

Preheat the oven to 170°C fan/340°F/gas 5 and line your 22 x 33 x 5cm (8½ x 13 x 2in) baking tray (sheet pan), see page 7.

Put the flour, baking powder, bicarbonate of soda (baking soda), mixed (pumpkin pie) spice, cinnamon and salt in a bowl, then add the butter and rub it in with your hands like you're making a crumble. Once you have that breadcrumb texture throughout, set aside and prep the apples.

Grate two of the apples into a bowl (skin too) and discard the core. Peel, core and cube the other three apples into pieces a little smaller than dice. Add the grated and diced apples to the crumble mix and mix through thoroughly, then add the honey and beaten eggs and bring it all together until you have a malleable batter. Press this into your baking tray, gently encouraging it into the corners.

To make the topping, peel and slice the three apples into thin strips so they look like crescent moons. Jauntily scatter these slices of apple over the top of the batter and sprinkle with the demerara sugar and a couple of pinches of cinnamon. Bake for 55–65 mins, or until you can stick a knife in the centre and it comes out clean. This is delicious served warm with clotted cream on the side.

The cake will keep for a week in an airtight container in the fridge.

After the bake, you can sprinkle over some more demerara sugar for extra crunch.

You can use sugar instead of honey if you like; use 400g (14oz) and add it at the crumble-making stage.

TECHNICAL

The following collection of recipes are a good way to give
your bakes a leg-up on to the pedestal where they belong, with
useful tips and recipes ranging from basic toppings to caramels,
candying and tempering. Some are super-quick and easy, and others
a little more challenging. It's a great reference point, not only
for the recipes in this book but for any baking you might turn
your hand to. There's no rule that says you have to do something
one way or another; you can switch up the toppings to use on many
of the cakes, whether it's because you want to make them dairy-
free, or just to mix things up a bit. It's worth noting that all
the recipes in this chapter are gluten-free. You'll find labels
for nut-free and vegan recipes throughout, as usual.

It's a good idea to invest in a thermometer with a detachable
probe, as a few of the recipes require temperature accuracy to
make them bang-on. When you're using a thermometer to check
things like caramel, it's a good idea to tilt the pan so the
melted sugar and golden syrup pool on one side and are deep
enough to take a temperature reading, otherwise the probe will
just touch the bottom of the pan, which is extremely hot.

BASIC FRUIT ICING

Bright-coloured fruit is a fun way to add some vibrancy and lift the appearance of the occasional sombre-looking bake. If the fruit you're using doesn't have seeds, you can simply blend it with some icing (confectioners') sugar to create a spreadable icing. If you do need to get rid of any pesky seeds, simply press the fruit through a sieve or stew it first in a little lemon juice and sugar to break it down, then sieve it to remove any gnarly bits.

MAKES ENOUGH TO TOP ONE CAKE
200–250g (7–9oz) icing (confectioners') sugar
50g (1¾oz) fresh raspberries
squeeze of lemon juice, if needed

VEGAN
NUT FREE

Gently sift the icing (confectioners') sugar into a bowl, then press the raspberries through a sieve over another bowl, using the back of a spoon to push them through. The juice will make its way through the sieve into the bowl. Remember to scrape the underside of the sieve, as that's where most of the juice will hang out.

Politely introduce the sifted sugar to the raspberry purée to avoid any drama, then stir to combine. If the icing is too thick, squeeze some lemon juice through the sieve to add some moisture and flush out any lingering raspberry juice that may have got away.

Use right away, or keep in the fridge in an airtight container for a week.

A smidgen of vanilla, orange or almond extract can give this icing an added spring in its step.

BASIC BUTTERCREAM

A basic recipe this may be, but it never fails to deliver the goods. A trained pastry chef might wave their whisk in despair and disagree, citing the fancier ways of professional kitchens. Sugar syrups, thermometers and eggs are used in the French and German methods, while the Swiss and Italian styles even incorporate meringue. Although clever, it can be a bit of a faff if you're just whipping up a cake in a small kitchen, and we believe in keeping things simple. The compromise with a basic buttercream is that the sugar ratio is higher, although that can be balanced out with a touch of acidic fruit. It can also develop a bit of a crust, which can be useful if you need to make a sturdier filling or shell.

MAKES ENOUGH TO FILL AND TOP ONE SANDWICH CAKE
250g (9oz) soft butter
500g (1lb 2oz) icing (confectioners') sugar
a few teaspoons of milk, fruit purée
  or other liquid flavourings

NUT FREE

Your butter must be at room temperature, or a little warmer, if possible. Pop it in a large mixing bowl or stand mixer with the sugar and beat for a couple of minutes until the mixture becomes pale, then add your chosen liquid to loosen the buttercream for ease of spreading and piping. Your chosen liquid will also add flavour and colour, be that fruit purée, vanilla, almond extract. If you want to keep it classic, then just add a splash of milk to help loosen it.

Use right away, or store in the fridge in an airtight container for a week. Allow to come up to room temperature and give it a mix before reusing.

YOGHURT DRIZZLE ICING

There is a bewildering alchemy that takes place when making a yoghurt icing: the more icing (confectioners') sugar you add, the runnier the mixture seems to become. We're no scientists, but it seems the sugar loosens the protein bonds that hold the water content of the yoghurt. To counter this, we like to go for a thick Greek yoghurt with 10 per cent fat. If you want to make a vegan version, use coconut yoghurt instead. Adding a squeeze of something sharp will tickle the taste buds, slapping away the saccharine nature of the sugar. To make this into a spreadable or pipeable icing, you will need to strain the yoghurt for a few hours beforehand, otherwise it's too runny.

MAKES ENOUGH TO TOP ONE CAKE
100g (3½oz) 10 per cent fat Greek yoghurt
  or coconut yoghurt
300g (10½oz) icing (confectioners') sugar
juice of ½ lime or lemon

NUT FREE

Place the yoghurt in a large mixing bowl and gently sift in the icing (confectioners') sugar, followed by the citrus juice. Gently fold everything together, trying not to kick up a dust storm with the powdered sugar.

Use right away, or keep in the fridge in an airtight container for a week.

WHIPPED CREAM ICING

The simple pleasure of whipping cream to top your sponge has probably been a bit lost with the availability of squirty cream; these days, it's easier to blast a can of mono-glycerides and nitrous oxide creaminess straight on to your cake, rather than work the wrists. But if you fancy going old school and making what the fancy folks call Chantilly cream, then here's how. This is just straight-up sweet whipped cream, but some vanilla is always invited.

MAKES ENOUGH TO TOP ONE CAKE
3–4 tablespoons icing (confectioners') sugar
  (about 30g/1oz)
300ml (10fl oz) double (heavy) cream, chilled

NUT FREE

Sift the icing (confectioners') sugar into a mixing bowl and add the cold cream. Then, using a whisk, simply whip the cream to soft peaks. Don't over-mix, or you'll end up with a crumbly and grainy looking mixture. (If this happens, just add a drop more cream; if you don't have any extra, a splash of milk will work too.)

If you're covering a cake with this cream, add fruit and a drizzle of berry juice over the top to make swirly patterns. Other fun embellishments include chocolate shavings, sprinkled nuts, a dusting of ground cardamom, or some grated nutmeg.

Use right away, or keep in the fridge in an airtight container for 3 days.

It's so easy to create variations of this: try adding orange or almond extract, or go boozy with something interesting like Frangelico, amaretto or kirsch. Whisky or brandy can give it a festive feel when that time of year comes around.

RICOTTA ICING

Often seen as the poor cousin to mascarpone, ricotta is certainly less luxurious, but does have a lightness that lends itself to a squeeze of citrus. The grainy texture isn't all bad; that scrappiness gives it character, making it perfect for a more rustic topping. Think of ricotta as linen and mascarpone as silk.

MAKES ENOUGH TO TOP ONE CAKE
150ml (5fl oz) double (heavy) cream
250g (9oz) ricotta
70g (2½oz) icing (confectioners') sugar

NUT FREE

In a large bowl, whip the cream until it creates pointy spikes when you lift the whisk out.

In a separate bowl, combine the ricotta and icing (confectioners') sugar until smooth, then fold together with the whipped cream.

The usual suspects can be added to this, such as vanilla, lemon zest or crumbled amaretti biscuits (cookies) for a bit of texture.

Use right away, or keep for 5 days in an airtight container in the fridge.

If you want to make a more traditional ricotta cream, ditch the double (heavy) cream and mix together four parts ricotta to one part caster (superfine) sugar and beat together.

MASCARPONE ICING

Mascarpone and Philadelphia cream cheese are quite different in texture, although when mixed, they hold each other with an acrobat's grip. There's something about Philadelphia – somehow it makes smoother and lighter icings; with this one, you'll pirouette and glide the palette knife over your cake like a ballerina.

MAKES ENOUGH TO TOP ONE CAKE
180g (6¼oz) cream cheese
  (we use Philadelphia)
250g (9oz) mascarpone
75g (2½oz) icing (confectioners') sugar

NUT FREE

Combine the cream cheese and mascarpone in a mixing bowl, then sift in the icing (confectioners') sugar and incorporate slowly to avoid getting enveloped in sweet clouds. Once it's gently combined, beat until smooth.

Use right away, or keep for 5 days in an airtight container in the fridge.

Add a little lemon juice and zest if you want to up the tempo and balance out any sweetness, or keep it classic with some vanilla extract. This will make enough icing to generously top one of our tray bakes.

YOGHURT GANACHE

This is a great alternative to using cream, and can balance out the sweetness of white chocolate or highlight the fruity acidity of a high-quality dark chocolate. If you're using really dark chocolate (over 70 per cent), though, the double acidity doesn't play well together, so cream is a better option. Using a thick Greek yoghurt is essential, as it has a lower water content, which will stop the ganache looking dull and opaque. To make a stiffer ganache, simply up the ratio of chocolate.

MAKES ENOUGH TO TOP ONE CAKE
200g (7oz) chocolate (fruity dark or white), broken into pieces
200g (7oz) Greek yoghurt

NUT FREE

Slowly melt the chocolate in a bain-marie (see page 8), then add the yoghurt, bit by bit, until the ganache has the desired consistency.

It will stiffen as it cools, and if the ganache has seized or become stiff too quickly, this is normally because the fats are getting on a bit too well. You can remedy this by placing the bowl back on the bain-marie with some gentle heat and aggressive whisking. If all else fails, hit the booze – seriously, a splash will revive your ganache and bring out a glossy glow.

Use right away, before the ganache stiffens.

To make a vegan version of this recipe, coconut cream or a little coconut oil works. Heat the oil, as you would the cream with a traditional ganache, then add to the chocolate chips, rather than following the method above, which melts the chocolate first.

CASHEW FROSTING

Usually, this kind of recipe is called 'cashew cream' and gets lumped in with the many free-from alternatives. We believe it shouldn't be hidden away under the 'dairy alternative' banner, but should instead be celebrated as a stand-alone topping, as it has true star quality. It's a real nut with real feelings, so give it some love – and time to soak.

MAKES ENOUGH TO TOP ONE CAKE
200g (7oz) cashews
50g (1¾oz) coconut oil
150ml (5fl oz) almond milk or other udderless milk
50g (1¾oz) maple syrup

VEGAN

Place the cashews in a bowl and cover with boiling water, then leave to soak for an hour or so. Or, if you prefer, you can soak them overnight in cold water. The nuts will swell up and put on a bit of weight, and this will help them blend to a smooth consistency.

Drain off the water and place the nuts in a blender with the coconut oil. (If the nuts are cold, melt the oil first.) Add the milk and syrup and keep blending through time and space, until you hit the milky way of creaminess.

Transfer the cream to the fridge to cool before using it as an icing. If it becomes too stiff, then whizz it up again with a splash more almond milk. The cream will keep in the fridge for a week or so; however when iced on a cake, it can dry out after a day, unless you keep the cake covered or in an airtight container.

COCONUT CREAM ICING

While the notion of a vegan cream icing might get a few eyes rolling, this one is a real banger and wouldn't be out of place used on non-vegan bakes, especially ones that pair well with coconut flavours. It would also make the basis of an amazing vegan ice cream with the addition of some sugar. The key here is to chill the cans of coconut milk before you start.

MAKES ENOUGH TO GENEROUSLY COVER A CAKE

2 x 400ml (14fl oz) cans of coconut milk, chilled overnight in the fridge or for 1 hour in the freezer
icing (confectioners') sugar (optional)

VEGAN

Take your chilled cans of coconut milk and open at the bottom. The liquid should have separated from the cream, so you can easily pour off the clear water. If you're in a situation where the cream and water are still a bit mixed up, strain through a fine sieve. Keep the water, as it makes a delicious drink.

Temperature plays a big part in the stiffness of this cream, so chilling your mixing bowl can also be useful on a hot day. Place the thick coconut cream from both cans into the (chilled) bowl and whisk until you reach the dizzy heights of soft peaks, with the solid cream becoming brilliantly white and silky.

A couple of tablespoons of icing (confectioners') sugar can be added; this loosens the mix slightly, which can be good if it's feeling a little stiff.

Spread directly on to your cooled cake, or serve alongside something warm. If the cream is too runny, chill it in the fridge or freezer to thicken up again; you might need to whip it into action once more before use.

Use right away, or keep for 5 days in an airtight container in the fridge.

Other sweeteners can be used, such as honey or agave syrup. The addition of vanilla is a cute bit of matchmaking. Depending on the cake you're using it with, a few drops of orange extract will give your icing some jazz hands.

TEMPERING CHOCOLATE

Tempering is all about making the chocolate look good, giving it a glossy finish with a snappy texture. Poorly tempered chocolate develops white streaks and, at worst, a mottled, mouldy appearance. If this happens, the poorly formed structure of the fat crystals also means it won't have that satisfying crack. Tempering is all about melting the chocolate on a low heat and quickly dropping its temperature before it solidifies. A thermometer is useful, and a general rule is to never heat your chocolate above 45°C (113°F).

The old-school method is to pour the chocolate on to a cool marble surface and scrape the melted mass around with a palette knife. These days, it's far easier to use the seed method, either in a bain-marie (see page 8) or in the microwave. This simply involves gently heating two thirds of the chocolate until melted, then stirring in the final third of solid chocolate, which then melts at the same time as bringing the temperature down.

If the temperature of the chocolate becomes too low, to the point that it's not workable, you can gently reheat it up to 30°C (86°F).

All chocolate will temper differently depending on the sugar and cocoa butter content, but the recipes below are a good starting point. There is some tolerance on the temperatures, so try not to stress about absolute accuracy.

A total of 300g (10½oz) chocolate is enough for a thin layer on any bakes made in the 22 x 33 x 5cm (8½ x 13 x 2in) baking tray (sheet pan), see page 7.

DARK CHOCOLATE

Melt two thirds of your chocolate pieces in a bain-marie (see page 8) or a bowl in a microwave to 42°C (108°F), constantly stirring with a spatula to avoid hot spots. Add the remaining third of your chocolate to bring the temperature down to around 29°C (84°F) with some vigorous stirring; decanting into a cooler bowl can also help. Then very gently bring the temperature back up to 34°C (93°F) to make the chocolate runny enough to use.

VEGAN
NUT FREE

WHITE CHOCOLATE

This is a little more temperamental than the dark stuff, but the principle is the same. First, melt two thirds of your chocolate pieces in a bain-marie (see page 8) or a bowl in a microwave to 38°C (100°F), constantly stirring with a spatula. Then, bit by bit, add the remaining third of your chocolate, constantly stirring to bring the temperature down to around 28°C (82°F). Then – very, very gently – bring the temperature back up to 32°C (89°F) before pouring, drizzling or dipping.

NUT FREE

PÂTES DE FRUITS

Probably better known as fruit pastels, these little nuggets of chewy joy are somewhere between a more forgiving jelly and a tougher fruit leather. They are delicious additions to any brownie mixture (see pages 46–77). The ratios are similar for most fruit, with equal parts sugar to fruit purée. The pectin determines the bite, the citric acid brings the acidity, and the glucose persuades the whole thing to stay together.

With pâtes de fruits, monitoring the temperature is the key to knowing whether you'll be getting a sticky mess or a perfectly set piece of fruit. The most important advice we can give you is to use a high-methoxyl pectin, which will stop things melting when heat is applied.

BLOOD ORANGE

Blood oranges are seasonal, so it's much easier to use a frozen block of fruit purée for this recipe. Boiron or Ponthier are two purée brands we can vouch for.

MAKES ABOUT 300G (10½oz)
500ml (17fl oz) blood orange juice or frozen fruit purée
400g (14oz) caster (superfine) sugar
15g (⅔oz) high-methoxyl yellow pectin (non-reversible)
100g (3½oz) glucose syrup
5g (1 teaspoon) citric acid
1 tablespoon water

VEGAN
NUT FREE

Line a baking tray (sheet pan) with greaseproof paper.

Heat the juice or purée in a heavy-based saucepan over a medium heat. In a small bowl, mix 50g (1¾oz) of the sugar with the powdered pectin and add this mixture to the pan, and whisk. Slowly add the rest of the sugar, along with the glucose syrup. Bubble away on the heat until it reaches 107°C (225°F).

In a small bowl, dilute the citric acid with the water, then add this to the pan and briefly whisk together. The acid will cause the mixture to seize up. Act quickly and tip the contents of the pan into your prepared tray. Leave to set for 1 hour. Once firm, cut the pâtes de fruits into your desired shapes.

This will keep for months in an airtight container in the fridge.

RASPBERRY

Bear in mind that the smaller the tray, the chunkier the cubes will be.

MAKES ABOUT 100G (3½oz)
150g (5¼oz) raspberries
110g (3¾oz) caster (superfine) sugar
3g high-methoxyl yellow pectin (non-reversible)
30g (1oz) glucose syrup
1g (¼ teaspoon) citric acid
½ teaspoon water

VEGAN
NUT FREE

Line a small loaf pan with siliconized baking parchment. Put the raspberries in a blender and whizz them into a purée, then strain through a sieve, pushing the pulp through with the back of a spoon.

Put the purée in a heavy-based saucepan over a medium–high heat. Mix 10g (½oz) of the caster (superfine) sugar with the pectin in a small jug and slowly add to the pan, whisking all the while. Next add the glucose, followed by the remaining sugar, continuing to whisk. Using a probe thermometer, heat the mixture to 107°C (225°F).

Meanwhile, rest a spoon on a flat surface and add the citric acid to the bowl of the spoon, then dissolve it by adding a few drops of water. Once the raspberry mixture is ready, add the citric acid mixture, briefly whisk together, then instantly pour this into the lined loaf pan. Leave to cool completely (this will take about half an hour), then slice into small cubes.

BASIC CARAMEL

There are two standard methods for making a basic caramel: wet and dry. Here, we go for the wet method, but we use lemon juice instead of water, as the acid helps to avoid crystallization. The dry method is made by melting sugar on its own. Both can produce the same results, but the dry method is perhaps a bit trickier, as the sugar can burn very quickly. This recipe will give a glass-like complexion to the caramel, which is great for creating shards or swirls to decorate your cakes.

MAKES ENOUGH TO TOP ONE CAKE

200g (7oz) caster (superfine) sugar
juice of ½ lemon

VEGAN
NUT FREE

Have a large bowl of cold water at the ready, big enough for your pan to be dunked in. Next, place the sugar in a heavy-based saucepan and squeeze in the lemon juice through a sieve to catch any bits. Place over a medium heat for a few minutes. You'll see the sugar around the edge of the pan turn to a transparent liquid. At this point, give the pan a gentle swirl to lift the liquified sugar off the bottom and allow the next layer of sugar to come into contact with the base of the pan. Keep doing this until all the sugar becomes liquid and starts to boil.

Keep boiling until the liquid sugar turns a dark amber colour. As soon as the temperature reaches 170°C (338°F), plunge the base of the pan into the cold water to halt the caramel – if it gets any hotter, you'll be burning the sugar.

Before the caramel sets, make your desired shapes, dip things into it, or spin it into fancy cages or nests. It's best to work on a sheet of baking parchment or a lightly oiled surface, as things can get sticky.

To clean the pan after making any type of caramel, just fill it with water and get it on the boil. This will dissolve any stubborn sugars.

It's best to use the caramel right away. If preparing in advance, keep in mind that the caramel will become soft and sticky over time

SOFT (SALTED) CARAMEL

This is probably the type of caramel you'll be most familiar with. Normally it's lightly salted, but we believe you can be a little more fearless with the salt if you're the gallant type. Finishing with an extra pinch of sea salt flakes will give the tongue a tickle, adding an extra layer of salty complexity. The soft caramel can be stored in a jar in the fridge and gently reheated if you want to make it runnier for pouring, or serving as a sauce. This is a more detailed version of the caramel recipe used for our Millionaire Brownie on page 66.

MAKES ENOUGH FOR ONE CAKE
100g (3½oz) golden syrup
100g (3½oz) sugar
150ml (5fl oz) double (heavy) cream
a pinch of salt
50g (1¾oz) butter

NUT FREE

Heat the golden syrup and sugar in a high-sided, heavy-based pan over a medium heat, until they have melted together and the mixture reaches 160°C (320°F) on the thermometer. Whisk in the cream and salt, along with 30g (1oz) of the butter, then increase the heat and keep things bubbling until the caramel reaches 117°C (243°F). At this point, it should become a deep golden colour. Remove from the heat, then whisk in the remaining 20g (¾oz) butter until well combined.

This is now ready to use, or you can pour it into a jar and keep in an airtight container in the fridge for 2 weeks.

FRENCH CARAMEL

This is a slight variation of our soft caramel recipe; the main difference is that this one resembles toffee: once set, it needs to be cut rather than scooped. The name is a gentle nod to the origins of salted caramel, which was originally made in Breton using salted butter. The burly result of this recipe enables it to be baked into a brownie (see page 69), where it will stand firm and really hold its shape rather than shirking its duty, giving up all hope of chewiness and fleeing into the mixture as things heat up. In this method, we've assumed you'll use it for brownies, but it can also be cut into cubes and hand-wrapped as a great homemade gift.

MAKES ENOUGH FOR ONE CAKE
80g (3oz) golden syrup
110g (3¾oz) sugar
100ml (3½fl oz) double (heavy) cream
a pinch of salt
40g (1½oz) butter

NUT FREE

Line a baking tray (sheet pan) with baking parchment.

Heat the golden syrup and sugar in a high-sided, heavy-based pan over a medium heat. When the caramel reaches 115°C (239°F), whisk in the cream and salt, along with 20g (¾oz) of the butter. Things can foam up at this point, which is why a high-sided pan is best.

Keep the pan on the heat and bring the temperature up to 127°C (261°F), then whisk in the remaining 20g (¾oz) butter and remove from the heat. Pour the hot caramel into the prepared tray. It will set quite quickly, but leave for an hour to cool before cutting.

Once cooled, slice into thin strips or cubes, ready to lay on top of your brownie mix before baking. You can also chop it up into small cubes and stir some into the brownie mix.

This will keep for 2 weeks in an airtight container in the fridge.

CANDIED NUTS

Most nuts benefit from being dressed up in a little jacket of shiny sweetness, then let loose to strut their stuff with a glistening twinkle. Some, like peanuts, lend themselves to a clout of salt, others to a dusting of cardamom, mixed (pumpkin pie) spice or cinnamon. We've kept it simple here by giving you a base recipe, leaving you free to jazz them up with whatever extra seasoning takes your fancy. There's no need to toast your nuts beforehand, as they will gain some toastiness during their makeover. Using golden syrup is a good shortcut, as the sugar is already halfway to becoming a dry caramel and will set firm. You can also vary the amount of syrup, depending on how shiny you want your nuts to be.

**MAKES ENOUGH TO TOP
ONE CAKE**
100g (3½oz) your chosen nuts
½–1 tablespoon golden syrup
a pinch of salt

VEGAN

Preheat the oven to 140°C fan/280°F/gas 3 and line a baking sheet with baking parchment.

Place the nuts on the prepared tray and drizzle the golden syrup over the top. Place in the oven and leave for 5 minutes. By that time, the syrup will be nice and runny, so turn the nuts over with a spatula until they're all covered in syrup.

Pop them back in the oven and repeat the process every 5 minutes until the syrup has become darker, thicker and generally more handsome. It's up to you how far you take things; just remember that different nuts caramelize at different rates, so keep a watchful eye. When you're happy with how they're looking, remove from the oven and spread them out before leaving to cool. This will prevent the nuts sticking together in clumps.

These can be stored in an airtight container for weeks, but be aware that they can become a bit sticky if abandoned for too long.

NUT OR SEED BRITTLES

The sheer variation of nuts and seeds you can use to make these means they are one of the most versatile recipes out there, yet they're also among the simplest. They can be paired up with almost any bake to add texture, flavour and a little flare. You can use various sugars, too: agave or maple add a different type of sweetness, while the addition of some zest or citrus juice will bring a little zing to proceedings.

Here, we've got a hard version and a chewy one. The hard brittle is easy to burn, so it's important to be bang-on with your timings. A gentle swirl is all that's needed to distribute the melting mass; don't agitate the sugars too much, otherwise you'll get crystallization. Hold your nerve, wait for the correct colour and temperature, then act quickly. With both types, using a white sugar helps you see how the caramelization is developing. Use your nose, too, sniffing out the whiff of toffee. If you smell any burning, you've gone too far. The carbon will pollute the whole flavour with an acrid undertone, so it'll be back to square one.

Never be tempted to touch the caramel or brittle with your hands until completely cool. Just when you think you can trust it, it's still too hot to handle.

CHEWY NUT BRITTLE

This is a chewier version of the hard brittle recipe, with an opaque finish and slight creaminess from the butter. This recipe calls for mixed nuts, but it's totally fine to use all the same, or you could even go for a mixture with seeds. Just take care when toasting them, as some will brown quicker than others.

MAKES ENOUGH TO TOP ONE CAKE
100g (3½oz) mixed nuts
100g (3½oz) caster (superfine) sugar
20g (¾oz) water
25g (1oz) butter
a pinch of sea salt flakes

Start by prepping a bowl of cold water big enough to fit your pan in and lay out a sheet of baking parchment.

Lightly toast the nuts in a dry frying pan (skillet) over a medium heat until they start to brown, then set aside.

Place the sugar and measured water in a heavy-based pan over a medium heat until the sugar dissolves and the mixture turns to syrup. Leave on the heat without stirring. When it becomes a nutty brown colour, add the butter and stir, then add the toasted nuts and mix so they're completely coated. The moment you see things turning nice and dark, dip the bottom of the pan in the waiting bowl of cold water, pulling the reins on the heat.

Tip the contents of the pan on to the baking parchment and spread things out. As the mass of nuttiness stiffens, sprinkle over the sea salt flakes, so they stick to the nearly set caramel.

This is delicious on its own, or can be used to add an extra dimension to a cake that's not hitting the spot.

This will keep in an airtight container for a few weeks, but will become sticky over time.

HARD CRACK BRITTLE

This method will give you a glass-like brittle that's perfect for cracking into shards to perch on top of your cakes. You can also smash it into tiny pieces to add a crunchy texture, either in the cake or scattered on top. In our recipe, we've used pistachios, but you can also dip toasted hazelnuts in the caramel to make glistening candied balls with tails like comets flying through the sky. If you wanted to transform this into sesame brittle, you might need to add 20ml (1½ tablespoons) of water to make the caramel less viscous, enabling it to get all up in those little seeds.

MAKES ENOUGH TO TOP ONE CAKE

100g (3½oz) caster (superfine) sugar
1 tablespoon honey
100g (3½oz) shelled pistachios

Have a bowl of cold water at the ready, big enough to fit the bottom of your pan in. Time is of the essence, and distractions can leave you with burnt caramel, or even a blistered hand. Preparation and concentration are your friends. Have a sheet of baking parchment laid out, ready to receive the cascade of nuts.

Heat the sugar and honey in a dry, heavy-based saucepan over a medium heat for a few minutes. You'll see the sugar begin to turn to a clear liquid and the honey start to melt. The sugar on top will remain in granular form, so tilt the pan to make a slope for the sugar to landslide into the honey. This is all the intervention needed. With eagle eyes, watch the bubbles erupt, billowing out puffs of steam, and wait for a glorious chestnut brown to develop.

As soon as it reaches the desired dark caramel colour, quickly add your nuts and mix with a spatula. If the pan is too hot and you're in fear of burning the sugar, dip the bottom of the pan in the bowl of cold water to cool it off. Keep mixing, then tip the contents on to the waiting sheet of baking parchment and spread it out with the spatula to cool.

This will keep for a few weeks in an airtight container, but will become sticky and softer over time.

CANDIED THINGS

Not only is candying a fun activity, for both adults and kids, it's also an inventive way of preserving a bumper crop or using up ingredients that might otherwise end up in the bin. Plus, of course, it's a good communicator. A delicate curl of candied carrot sitting on top of a frosted carrot cake is the baker's version of a bumper sticker that says 'Carrots on board'; the same goes for candied lemon on a lemon cake, and so on.

CANDIED BEETS, CARROTS, APPLES & FIRM PEARS

With this process, you're simply removing the water and replacing it with sugar. There are a few different ways to do this; we've stuck to a simple method using trays in the oven. It starts with an initial cooking process to break down the cell walls and release the water, then it's a case of dehydrating things to remove the water, turning the slices into something fragile and beautiful. Courgettes (zucchinis) or squash can be manipulated in this fashion too.

The objective is not to caramelize the sugars, so if your oven tends to run a little hot, play it safe and try this on a lower temperature the first time; it might just mean you have to bake them for longer.

MAKES ENOUGH TO TOP ONE OR TWO CAKES

carrots, beets, apples or firm pears
(1 or 2 of each is plenty)
200g (7oz) caster (superfine) sugar

Two baking trays (sheet pans) are useful for this recipe, but not essential; you could also use a baking sheet.

VEGAN
NUT FREE

Preheat the oven to 90°C fan/200°F/gas ¼ and line two 22 x 33 x 5cm (8½ x 13 x 2in) baking trays (sheet pans), see page 7.

Slice your chosen crop as thinly as possible, ideally about 1mm (⅛in) thick. A mandoline is great for this, but if you don't have one, use your samurai skills with a knife. Place the sugar in a bowl or on a plate and dip each slice in the sugar to coat both sides, then place on the prepared tray, leaving a gap between the slices. Lay another sheet of baking parchment over the top of the slices, then press a second baking tray on top to weigh it down. Bake between the two baking trays for 25–30 minutes. Remove from the oven and uncover the goods, carefully peeling back the top layer of baking parchment. Pat off any excess moisture with some paper towel (beetroot juice will make a bid for freedom, turning everything pink), then return to the oven, uncovered, and bake for 1–2 hours at about 80°C fan/170°F/gas <¼. The thinner slices will be ready first.

When they emerge from the oven, the slices will still be a little soft and flexible, so leave to cool on the baking tray and dry out a little more to gain some snap. They will remain in this form for about 3 days, after which they'll begin to soften up – but you can just pop them back in a low oven for a few minutes to crisp up again.

These will keep for months in an airtight container.

QUASI CANDIED CITRUS

This is a shortcut version of candying citrus, and although this imitation is edible, it's geared more towards decoration than trying to emulate the real deal, which can take months to make properly. This recipe is pretty much the same as our other candying method (see page 155), but involves a slightly higher temperature to initially cook off the peel, and a longer dehydration time to remove any chewiness. This method will work with pineapple and kiwi fruit, too – just be sure to remove the skin.

MAKES ENOUGH TO TOP ONE OR TWO CAKES
your chosen citrus fruits, ideally
   unwaxed (3 or 4 is plenty)
200g (7oz) caster (superfine) sugar

You will need two baking trays
   (sheet pans) for this recipe

VEGAN
NUT FREE

Preheat the oven to 120°C fan/250°F/gas 1 and line your 22 x 33 x 5cm (8½ x 13 x 2in) baking tray (sheet pan), see page 7.

If you can't get hold of unwaxed citrus, give your chosen fruit a good scrub in water first, as you won't be peeling the fruit. With a good, sharp knife, slice your citrus into rounds about 2mm (⅟₁₆in) thick, cutting across the centre so they look like bicycle wheels. Remove any pips. Place the sugar in a bowl or on a plate and dip the slices in the sugar, coating both sides, then lay on the prepared tray, leaving a gap between the slices.

Lay another sheet of baking parchment over the top of the slices, then press a second baking tray on top to weigh it down. Bake between the two baking trays for 15–20 minutes to cook off the fruit and release the moisture. Remove from the oven and dab away any excess juice with some paper towels; there can be rather a lot. Return the tray to the oven, uncovered, and bake 2–2½ hours at 80°C fan/170°F/gas <¼. The thinner slices will be ready first.

These will keep for months in an airtight container.

Use these to decorate your bakes, with half wheels sticking out of the top of cakes or whole slices laid flat on icing. They can be a fun way to jazz up a cocktail glass, too, and can even be used for decorations at Christmas. If you have the peel from a citrus fruit going to waste, you can candy it with this same method, then add it to cake mixes for a boost of flavour.

ELDERFLOWER SYRUP

Although elderflower cordial is readily available in supermarkets, it's just a watered-down imitation of the real deal. Part of the joy of this drink is the sunny day spent picking the elderflowers, teetering on a wobbly ladder and clutching a scrunched-up old carrier bag to hold your bounty. It's a fun day out and adds a bit of story to your recipes in a way that a trip to Tesco never could. Get out there in summer and hunt some elderflowers down; just avoid the ones near busy roads, as the pollution will probably have got to them first. Adding citric acid does add flavour, but it will also preserve the cordial. We use this recipe in our Gooseberry and Elderflower Cake on page 86, but it can also be used to bring some early summer stylings to other cakes – try adding it to the icing for sponges or adding some to the syrup for drizzle cakes.

MAKES ABOUT 3 LITRES
(101 FL OZ)
20–30 fresh elderflower heads
2 litres (70fl oz) water
1kg (2lb 4oz) caster
 (superfine) sugar
finely grated zest and juice of
 3–4 lemons
20g (¾oz) citric acid (optional)

VEGAN
NUT FREE

After picking, remove as much stalk from the elderflower heads as possible and set aside.

Heat the water and sugar in a large, heavy-based saucepan over a high heat until the water boils and the sugar dissolves. Add the lemon zest and juice, along with the citric acid (if using), followed by all the elderflower heads. Take off the heat, cover the hot pan and leave overnight to infuse.

The next day, strain the liquid by passing it through a fine mesh sieve. If you used the citric acid, you can bottle it up, label it and store it in the fridge for a couple of weeks. Alternatively, if you made it without the citric acid, you can freeze it until needed. Delicious as a drink, in cakes, or in salad dressings, too.

INDEX

ACKNOWLEDGEMENTS

OLIVER

The initial phone call about writing this book blindsided me. I was holding the phone, staring at yet another broken dishwasher in our café and trying to organize fixing a leak at our bakery, wondering which one I should prioritize and why I'd started a company so heavily reliant on water and pipework, without having done a plumbing course first. I said there's no way we have the time or skills needed to write a book, but after a few more conversations and some time, I was convinced; it's not everyday you get to become an author. So, thank you, to our commissioning editor Céline, for giving us the confidence to put this book out there.

As the project got going, we realized the size of the task, and turned to friends who we knew had been there before. In moments of crisis, Clare Lattin, from Ducksoup, always pointed us in the right direction.

Thanks to Jack Adair Bevan, who spent an afternoon with me drinking beers and giving advice on how to cope with imposter syndrome.

The biggest thanks to all our staff for stepping up, holding the fort and giving us the time to write and test the recipes.

An extra special thank you to my lovely wife Victoria, for giving me the time and headspace to untangle my mind and put some of my brain on the page.

Also to my daughter Agatha, for not putting all your toys in daddy's shed, which was the only place I could concentrate on writing.

Then lastly my co-author, business partner, and dearest friend Tom, you're a cracking writer, but most of all, thanks for tolerating my difficult personality and nurturing the best of me. You managed to straighten out my meandering sentences into words with direction towards cake, rather than waffle.

TOM

It's not often you get the stage to publicly thank people for their help and support, and since I'm unlikely to ever win an Oscar, I'll take this as my opportunity and I assure you that I am crying whilst typing.

Firstly to my Mum, Elaine, for inspiring me to bake so many years ago and for instilling a family culture of good food right from the off.

To my partner Emily, for being there with unlimited support and positive encouragement.

To all the friends who politely nodded along to my endless chat about the monotony of recipe editing and tweaking.

Thanks to the ever fastidious Will Perrens, for laying the brilliant design foundations of the book and for all the honest feedback and advice.

To Jess McIntosh, for going the extra mile on the photoshoot, working so hard and baking up a storm, and doing it all with a smile, and to Becks Wilkinson for the amazingly precise planning and the sheer amount of work you got through on the food styling.

Thanks to Ola Smit for the studio space and to Sam Harris and Matt Hague for utilizing the natural light so well in creating the knockout photography.

A big thank you to our editor Stacey, for guiding us through the process, putting up with our constant creative pushbacks and then picking up our toys when we threw them out of the pram, all done with a brilliantly dry sense of humour and an eye for the bigger picture.

Finally, a huge thank you to Oliver, for remaining a friend first and business partner second and always encouraging me to step out of my comfort zone just the right amount. You dragged this book to life with your relentless creativity, infectious energy and some pretty maverick humour, some of which may be lost to the cutting room floor, but certainly made the writing process a whole load of fun.